EVERY DAY FAVOURITES

Canadian Living

COOKBOOK

TRANSCONTINENTAL BOOKS INC.

1100 René-Lévesque Blvd. West

24th Floor

Montreal (Quebec) H3B 4X9

Tel.: 514 392-9000

Toll free: 1 800 361-5479

www.livres.transcontinental.ca

—

Distribution in Canada

Random House of Canada

2775 Matheson Blvd East

Mississauga, Ontario

L4W 4P7

—

Library and Archives Canada Cataloguing in Publication

Main entry under title :

EVERYDAY FAVOURITES

Includes index.

ISBN-13: 978-0-9738355-0-8

ISBN-10: 0-9738355-0-8

1. Cookery. I. Canadian Living Test Kitchen. II. Canadian Living.

TX714.E93 2005   641.5   C2005-941640-8

—

Senior editor: Beverley Renahan

Cover: photography, Hasnain Dattu; food styling, Julie Aldis; props styling, Oksana Slavutych

Illustrations: Michael Erb

Cover page design and graphic concept: orangetango

—

—

Printed in Canada

© Transcontinental Books, 2005

Legal deposit — 3rd Quarter 2005

National Library of Quebec

National Library of Canada

ISBN-13: 978-0-9738355-0-8

ISBN-10: 0-9738355-0-8

—

We acknowledge the financial support of our publishing activity

by the Government of Canada through the BPDIP program

of the Department of Canadian Heritage, as well as by the Government of Québec

through the SODEC program Aide à la promotion.

In The Canadian Living Test Kitchen, we get a buzz creating dishes for special occasions: a Thai feast for friends, a Halloween party or a "love"ly dinner for Valentine's Day. But even we foodies have to admit that when it comes to significance, special-occasion cooking pales in comparison to everyday cooking.

Food is the glue of family life, regulating and calming its daily pulse; it brings together and cements communities, and defines cultures. No, I don't suggest that eating spaghetti belies an Italian heritage, or that a fondness for butter tarts pegs you as Canadian. I mean that the togetherness, the warm memories of laughs and lives shared around dishes that get made over and over again – steak with smoky barbecue sauce, crispy chicken fingers, chocolate cheesecake – help define who we are.

Favourite and shared meals, whether Friday-night pizza at home, the annual block-party burgers or Thanksgiving's heavenly sage-stuffed turkey, ground us to siblings, parents, kids, grandparents, tradition and heritage. They give us collective memories – not just of the aromas, textures and tastes of the food, but of each other. They focus our days. Dinner (or supper) means, yes, a tasty meal; but it's also time to talk, to share anxieties and triumphs and to pass on stories and traditions.

Yes, we know that with commutes, soccer games, dance lessons, homework and overtime, sharing a family – let alone a community – meal isn't always easy. We also realize, as you do, that home cooking is healthy, budget-friendly and bond-building. And that's where The Canadian Living Test Kitchen comes in: to help put those benefits within reach while accommodating the demands of busy lives.

Over the past 30 years, *Canadian Living* Magazine has established itself as a kitchen staple: a beloved and invaluable tool for everyday Canadian cooks. In our kitchens, which look just like yours (no fancy restaurant stoves or superhot grills for us), we aim to make cooking easy, quick, healthy and affordable – never forgetting, of course, that it has to be delicious, first and foremost.

As we celebrate our 30th anniversary, we want to bring you good health, happiness, success and the fundamental pleasure of sharing good food together.

Elizabeth Baird

Elizabeth Baird — Food Editor, *Canadian Living* Magazine

TABLE OF CONTENTS

← 11

CHAPTER 1
SOUPS

CARROT AND RED LENTIL SOUP WITH PARSLEY CREAM

Easy, delicious and simple but comforting, this soup is just right for either family or company. In a hurry? Skip the garnish and top the soup with croutons.

Makes 4 to 6 servings

2 tbsp	extra-virgin olive oil	25 mL
3 cups	sliced carrots (about 1 lb/500 g)	750 mL
1	onion, chopped	1
1	small sweet red pepper, chopped	1
2	cloves garlic, minced	2
2 tsp	ground ginger	10 mL
6 cups	chicken stock	1.5 L
1 cup	red lentils, sorted and rinsed	250 mL
2 tsp	lemon juice	10 mL
¼ tsp	salt	1 mL
PARSLEY CREAM		
½ cup	fresh parsley leaves	125 mL
1	green onion	1
⅓ cup	sour cream	75 mL
Pinch	cayenne pepper	Pinch

← In large saucepan, heat oil over medium heat; fry carrots, onion, red pepper, garlic and ginger, stirring often, for 5 minutes.

← Add stock and lentils; bring to boil. Reduce heat, cover and simmer until carrots are tender, 15 to 20 minutes.

← With immersion blender or in batches in blender, purée soup; return to simmer. Season with lemon juice and salt.

← **PARSLEY CREAM:** Meanwhile, finely chop parsley and green onion; place in small bowl. Mix in sour cream and cayenne pepper.

← Ladle soup into bowls; garnish each with spoonful of Parsley Cream.

PER EACH OF 6 SERVINGS: about 256 cal, 15 g pro, 8 g total fat (2 g sat. fat), 32 g carb, 7 g fibre, 934 mg sodium. % RDI: 7% calcium, 33% iron, 191% vit A, 53% vit C, 90% folate.

SUCCOTASH SOUP

This corn, bean and squash soup takes 15 minutes to make yet offers a fabulous bowl of flavour and satisfaction.

Makes 6 servings

1 tbsp	vegetable oil	15 mL
1 cup	chopped peeled squash	250 mL
1	onion, chopped	1
2	cloves garlic, minced	2
1	each carrot and stalk celery, chopped	1
½ tsp	each dried thyme and pepper	2 mL
4 cups	chicken stock	1 L
1	can (28 oz/796 mL) diced tomatoes	1
1 cup	frozen corn kernels	250 mL
1 cup	frozen lima beans	250 mL

⬅ In saucepan, heat oil over medium heat; cook squash, onion, garlic, carrot, celery, thyme and pepper, stirring occasionally, until softened, about 10 minutes.

⬅ Add stock, tomatoes, corn and lima beans; bring to boil. Reduce heat, cover and simmer until beans are hot.

PER SERVING: about 150 cal, 8 g pro, 4 g total fat (1 g sat. fat), 24 g carb, 4 g fibre, 0 mg chol, 742 mg sodium. % RDI: 7% calcium, 16% iron, 57% vit A, 43% vit C, 15% folate.

DIJON GRILLED CHEESE

This old favourite gets more interesting with a little mustard and nutritious chewy bread.

⬅17

Makes 4 servings

1 tbsp	Dijon mustard	15 mL
8	slices walnut, oatmeal or whole grain bread	8
4	thin slices cheese	4
2 tsp	butter	10 mL

⬅ Spread mustard over 4 of the bread slices; top each with cheese slice. Cover each with bread slice. Spread outside of each with ½ tsp (2 mL) butter.

⬅ In skillet, fry sandwiches over medium heat, pressing gently with spatula, until golden brown and cheese melts, about 4 minutes. (Or toast in sandwich press or grill.)

PER SERVING: about 378 cal, 13 g pro, 15 g total fat (7 g sat. fat), 46 g carb, 5 g fibre, 36 mg chol, 1,102 mg sodium. % RDI: 24% calcium, 18% iron, 6% vit A, 20% folate.

BEEF AND NOODLE SOUP

Hints of orange and ginger add Asian sparkle to this filling soup.

Makes 4 servings

1 tbsp	vegetable oil	**15 mL**
12 oz	top sirloin grilling steak, thinly sliced	**375 g**
2	cloves garlic, thinly sliced	**2**
½ tsp	grated orange rind	**2 mL**
¼ tsp	ground ginger	**1 mL**
Pinch	each cinnamon, ground fennel seeds and hot pepper flakes	**Pinch**
3 cups	beef stock	**750 mL**
2 tbsp	soy sauce	**25 mL**
4 oz	fettuccine	**125 g**
4 cups	spinach leaves, trimmed	**1 L**
2	green onions, thinly sliced	**2**

← In large saucepan, heat oil over medium-high heat; brown beef, in batches, about 2 minutes. Remove and set aside.

← Add garlic, orange rind, ginger, cinnamon, ground fennel seeds and hot pepper flakes to pan; fry over medium heat until fragrant, about 1 minute.

← Add stock and 2 cups (500 mL) water; bring to boil. Reduce heat and simmer for 8 minutes, skimming off any foam. Stir in soy sauce.

← Meanwhile, in large pot of boiling salted water, cook fettuccine until tender but firm, about 10 minutes. Drain.

← Divide fettuccine, beef and spinach among soup bowls. Add stock mixture; sprinkle with onions.

PER SERVING: about 277 cal, 26 g pro, 8 g total fat (2 g sat. fat), 25 g carb, 3 g fibre, 40 mg chol, 1,266 mg sodium. % RDI: 10% calcium, 36% iron, 44% vit A, 12% vit C, 60% folate.

CHICKEN TORTILLA SOUP

There are chicken soups from all cultures, and this zingy and colourful example puts a taste of Mexico on your table.

Makes 6 servings

3	boneless skinless chicken breasts	3
4	corn tortillas (about 4 inches/10 cm)	4
2 tbsp	vegetable oil	25 mL
2	cloves garlic, minced	2
1	onion, chopped	1
1 tsp	ground cumin	5 mL
¼ tsp	chili powder	1 mL
1	each sweet red and yellow pepper, chopped	1
4	plum tomatoes, chopped	4
4 cups	chicken stock	1 L
1 cup	corn kernels	250 mL
1 tbsp	lime juice	15 mL
¼ cup	chopped fresh coriander	50 mL

← Cut chicken diagonally into ¼-inch (5 mm) thick strips; set aside.

← Cut tortillas into ¼-inch (5 mm) thick strips. In large wide saucepan, heat 1 tbsp (15 mL) of the oil over medium-high heat; fry tortilla strips, stirring, until crisp, about 2 minutes. With slotted spoon, transfer to paper towels to drain.

← Add remaining oil, garlic, onion, cumin and chili powder to pan; fry over medium heat, stirring occasionally, until softened, about 3 minutes.

← Add chicken and red and yellow peppers; fry until chicken is golden, about 5 minutes. Add tomatoes and stock; bring to boil. Reduce heat and simmer for 7 minutes.

← Add corn; cook for 2 minutes. Stir in lime juice. Ladle into bowls; garnish with tortilla chips and coriander.

PER SERVING: about 207 cal, 21 g pro, 7 g total fat (1 g sat. fat), 16 g carb, 2 g fibre, 39 mg chol, 576 mg sodium. % RDI: 4% calcium, 11% iron, 12% vit A, 120% vit C, 16% folate.

RUBY RED BORSCHT

Prairie-Ukrainian heritage is served up in a bowlful of borscht. It's chock-full of tender vegetables and topped with sour cream and dill.

Makes 8 servings

4	small beets with tops	4
1 cup	shredded cabbage	250 mL
1	onion, chopped	1
1	potato, peeled and chopped	1
1	small carrot, chopped	1
1	small stalk celery, chopped	1
½ cup	chopped green beans	125 mL
6 cups	chicken or vegetable stock	1.5 L
¼ cup	ketchup or tomato juice	50 mL
¼ cup	sour cream	50 mL
1 tbsp	all-purpose flour	15 mL
1 tbsp	lemon juice	15 mL
Pinch	pepper	Pinch
2 tbsp	chopped fresh dill	25 mL
	Sour cream	
	Fresh dill sprigs	

← Cut off beet greens and stems. Shred greens and set aside. Peel beets; chop stems. ← 23

← In large stockpot, combine beets and stems, cabbage, onion, potato, carrot, celery and green beans. Pour in stock and ketchup; bring to boil. Cover and simmer until vegetables are tender-crisp, about 40 minutes.

← In small bowl, whisk together sour cream, flour, lemon juice and pepper; stir into soup. Stir in beet greens; cook for 15 minutes. Stir in chopped dill.

← Ladle soup into bowls; garnish each with spoonful of sour cream and dill sprigs.

PER SERVING: about 94 cal, 6 g pro, 2 g total fat (1 g sat. fat), 14 g carb, 2 g fibre, 3 mg chol, 750 mg sodium. % RDI: 5% calcium, 9% iron, 27% vit A, 18% vit C, 16% folate.

SQUASH AND ONION SOUP GRATINÉE

This crusty-topped soup may have started out as French onion, but the chunks of squash have added a satisfying Canadian touch. If you buy a slim baguette, top the soup with three slices, as we did in our photo.

Makes 6 servings

2 tbsp	butter	25 mL
4	onions, thinly sliced	4
1 tbsp	all-purpose flour	15 mL
1 tsp	chopped fresh thyme (or ½ tsp/2 mL dried)	5 mL
½ tsp	pepper	2 mL
Pinch	grated nutmeg	Pinch
5 cups	beef stock	1.25 L
1 cup	apple cider	250 mL
2 tsp	cider vinegar	10 mL
3 cups	cubed peeled butternut squash	750 mL
12	baguette slices (¾ inch/2 cm thick)	12
2 cups	shredded aged Gouda or Gruyère cheese	500 mL

← In large saucepan, melt butter over medium-low heat; fry onions, stirring occasionally, until evenly golden, about 20 minutes.

← Stir in flour, thyme, pepper and nutmeg; cook, stirring, for 1 minute. Add stock, apple cider and vinegar; bring to boil. Reduce heat; cover and simmer for 20 minutes.

← Add squash; cover and simmer until tender, about 12 minutes. *Make-ahead: Let cool for 30 minutes. Refrigerate, uncovered, in airtight container until cold; cover and refrigerate for up to 24 hours.*

← Ladle into 6 ovenproof French onion soup bowls or heatproof bowls; top each with 2 baguette slices, then cheese. Bake on rimmed baking sheet in 400°F (200°C) oven until cheese is bubbly and lightly browned, about 18 minutes.

PER SERVING: about 347 cal, 16 g pro, 16 g total fat (10 g sat. fat), 37 g carb, 3 g fibre, 54 mg chol, 1,180 mg sodium. % RDI: 32% calcium, 15% iron, 65% vit A, 25% vit C, 27% folate.

PASTA
E FAGIOLI

26 →

It's worth it to buy a chunk of real
Parmigiano-Reggiano to grate over the soup.
Romano is a top-notch substitute.

Makes 6 servings

1 tbsp	extra-virgin olive oil	**15 mL**
1	onion, chopped	**1**
2	cloves garlic, minced	**2**
2	stalks celery, chopped	**2**
2	carrots, chopped	**2**
5 cups	chicken stock	**1.25 L**
1	can (28 oz/796 mL) diced tomatoes	**1**
½ cup	diced prosciutto or Black Forest ham (about 3 oz/90 g)	**125 mL**
¾ cup	tubetti or other small pasta (3 oz/90 g)	**175 mL**
1	can (19 oz/540 mL) romano beans, drained and rinsed	**1**
¼ tsp	pepper	**1 mL**
2 tbsp	grated Parmesan cheese	**25 mL**

← In large saucepan or Dutch oven, heat oil over medium heat; fry onion, garlic, celery and carrots, stirring often, until onion is softened, about 5 minutes.

← Add stock, 1 cup (250 mL) water, tomatoes and prosciutto; bring to boil. Reduce heat and simmer until vegetables are tender, about 30 minutes. *Make-ahead: Let cool for 30 minutes. Refrigerate, uncovered, in airtight container until cold; cover and refrigerate for up to 2 days or freeze for up to 2 weeks. Reheat to proceed.*

← Add pasta; cook until tender but firm, 6 to 8 minutes. Add romano beans and pepper; heat through. Ladle into bowls; sprinkle with Parmesan.

PER SERVING: about 274 cal, 17 g pro, 6 g total fat (2 g sat. fat), 39 g carb, 7 g fibre, 9 mg chol, 1,302 mg sodium. % RDI: 10% calcium, 21% iron, 69% vit A, 25% vit C, 38% folate.

WONTON SOUP

Frozen wontons, already stuffed with pork or shrimp, make this restaurant dish a quick soup.

Makes 4 servings

4 cups	chicken stock	1 L
2	heads baby bok choy	2
2 cups	sliced mushrooms	500 mL
1	pkg (300 g) frozen pork or shrimp wontons	1
1 cup	bean sprouts	250 mL
1	carrot, shredded	1
3	green onions, sliced	3
¼ cup	coriander or parsley leaves	50 mL

←29

← In large saucepan, bring stock and 2 cups (500 mL) water to boil. Cut bok choy lengthwise into quarters; add to stock. Add mushrooms; reduce heat, cover and simmer for 10 minutes.

← Add wontons; cook over medium-high heat, covered, until wontons float to surface, about 4 minutes.

← Add bean sprouts, carrot, green onions and coriander.

PER SERVING: about 228 cal, 14 g pro. 5 g total fat (1 g sat. fat), 32 g carb, 3 g fibre, 12 mg chol, 1,185 mg sodium. % RDI: 9% calcium, 25% iron, 58% vit A, 32% vit C, 39% folate.

QUICK FISHERMAN'S STEW

30 → Frozen mixed cooked seafood gives this whole supper soup a variety of tastes. But you can use an equal amount of cubed raw fish and simmer until the fish flakes when tested, a few minutes longer than the cooked seafood.

Makes 4 to 6 servings

1 tbsp	vegetable oil	**15 mL**
1	onion, chopped	**1**
3 cups	diced potatoes	**750 mL**
1 cup	chopped carrots	**250 mL**
1	sweet green pepper, chopped	**1**
2	cloves garlic, minced	**2**
1 tsp	dried thyme	**5 mL**
½ tsp	each salt and pepper	**2 mL**
1	can (28 oz/796 mL) diced tomatoes	**1**
1	bottle (240 mL) clam juice	**1**
1	pkg (340 g) frozen mixed cooked seafood, thawed and drained	**1**
2 tbsp	minced fresh parsley	**25 mL**
2	green onions, thinly sliced	**2**

← In saucepan, heat oil over medium heat; fry onion, potatoes, carrots, green pepper, garlic, thyme, salt and pepper, stirring often, until onion and pepper are softened, about 6 minutes.

← Add tomatoes, clam juice and 1 cup (250 mL) water; bring to boil. Reduce heat, cover and simmer until potatoes are tender, about 20 minutes.

← Add seafood; simmer, covered, until hot, about 4 minutes. Stir in parsley and green onions.

PER EACH OF 6 SERVINGS: about 180 cal, 12 g pro, 3 g total fat (trace sat. fat), 26 g carb, 3 g fibre, 66 mg chol, 617 mg sodium. % RDI: 9% calcium, 26% iron, 59% vit A, 73% vit C, 15% folate.

GARLIC CROÛTES

These partner particularly well with stew or soup.

Makes 8 pieces

2	cloves garlic, minced	**2**
2 tbsp	minced fresh parsley	**25 mL**
2 tbsp	extra-virgin olive oil	**25 mL**
8	slices baguette	**8**

← In small bowl, mix together garlic, parsley and oil; spread over baguette slices. Arrange on rimmed baking sheet; broil until golden, about 1 minute.

PER PIECE: about 72 cal, 1 g pro, 4 g total fat (1 g sat. fat), 8 g carb, 1 g fibre, 0 mg chol, 92 mg sodium. % RDI: 1% calcium, 4% iron, 2% vit C, 7% folate.

INGREDIENTS: WATER,
MUSTARD SEEDS, VINEGAR,
SALT, POTASSIUM
METABISULPHITE, CITRIC ACID.

INGREDIENTS: EAU,
GRAINES DE MOUTARDE,
VINAIGRE, SEL, METABISULFITE
DE POTASSIUM, ACIDE CITRIQUE.

Stir well before using.
Bien mélanger avant utilisation.

Refrigerate after opening.
Tenir au frais après ouverture.

34 →

CHAPTER 2
SALADS

FENNEL AND CABBAGE COLESLAW

38 → Fennel gives this coleslaw an added crunch and a hint of licorice. If you have one, use a mandoline to slice the hard vegetables paper-thin.

Makes 8 servings

4 cups	finely shredded green cabbage	1 L
4	green onions, thinly sliced	4
2	stalks celery, thinly sliced	2
1	large carrot, finely diced	1
Half	fennel bulb, thinly sliced	Half
Half	sweet red pepper, thinly sliced	Half
DRESSING		
⅓ cup	Homemade Salad Dressing (recipe, this page) or light mayonnaise	75 mL
⅓ cup	light sour cream	75 mL
1 tbsp	each Dijon mustard and cider vinegar	15 mL
2 tsp	granulated sugar	10 mL
½ tsp	each salt, pepper and celery or mustard seeds	2 mL

← In large bowl, toss together cabbage, onions, celery, carrot, fennel and red pepper. *Make-ahead: Cover with damp towel and plastic wrap; refrigerate for up to 8 hours.*

← **DRESSING:** In small bowl, stir together Homemade Salad Dressing, sour cream, mustard, vinegar, sugar, salt, pepper and celery seeds; scrape over cabbage mixture and toss to coat evenly. *Make-ahead: Cover and refrigerate for up to 2 hours.*

PER SERVING: about 67 cal, 2 g pro, 1 g total fat (1 g sat. fat), 13 g carb, 2 g fibre, 6 mg chol, 260 mg sodium. % RDI: 6% calcium, 5% iron, 42% vit A, 60% vit C, 16% folate.

HOMEMADE SALAD DRESSING

Use this old-fashioned sweet and tangy cooked dressing for tuna, egg, potato and chicken salads, too.

Makes about 2 cups (500 mL)

1 cup	granulated sugar	250 mL
2 tbsp	all-purpose flour	25 mL
2 tsp	dry mustard	10 mL
1 tsp	salt	5 mL
Pinch	turmeric	Pinch
1	egg	1
1 cup	cider vinegar	250 mL
1 cup	milk	250 mL
1 tbsp	butter	15 mL

← In top of double boiler or in heavy saucepan, whisk together sugar, flour, mustard, salt and turmeric. Whisk in egg, vinegar, milk and butter.

← Cook over simmering water or over medium-low heat, stirring constantly, until thick enough to coat back of spoon, 10 to 15 minutes. Let cool, stirring often. Dressing will thicken when cooling. *Make-ahead: Refrigerate in airtight container for up to 1 month.*

PER 1 TBSP (15 mL): about 37 cal, 1 g pro, 1 g total fat (trace sat. fat), 7 g carb, 0 g fibre, 7 mg chol, 81 mg sodium. % RDI: 1% calcium, 1% iron, 1% vit A, 1% folate.

CHICKPEA TABBOULEH SALAD

We like to warm pita breads to serve with this vegetarian main course salad.

Makes 4 servings

1 cup	medium or coarse bulgur	250 mL
1	can (19 oz/540 mL) chickpeas, drained and rinsed	1
2	tomatoes, seeded and chopped	2
1 cup	diced English cucumber	250 mL
1 cup	minced fresh Italian parsley	250 mL
½ cup	chopped green onions	125 mL
¼ cup	chopped fresh mint	50 mL
DRESSING		
¼ cup	lemon juice	50 mL
2 tbsp	extra-virgin olive oil	25 mL
2	cloves garlic, minced	2
1 tsp	salt	5 mL
½ tsp	pepper	2 mL

← In saucepan, bring 1¾ cups (425 mL) water to boil; stir in bulgur. Reduce heat to low; cover and cook until no liquid remains, about 10 minutes. Transfer to large bowl; fluff with fork. Let cool to room temperature.

← Add chickpeas, tomatoes, cucumber, parsley, onions and mint.

← **DRESSING:** In small bowl, whisk together lemon juice, oil, garlic, salt and pepper; pour over bulgur mixture and toss to combine.

← 41

PER SERVING: about 336 cal, 13 g pro, 9 g total fat (1 g sat. fat), 56 g carb, 9 g fibre, 0 mg chol, 803 mg sodium. % RDI: 3% calcium, 29% iron, 14% vit A, 50% vit C, 56% folate.

TIP

For nonvegetarians, substitute 1 lb (500 g) peeled and deveined grilled large shrimp or chicken strips for the chickpeas.

RED POTATO AND RADISH SALAD

Potato salad is a Canadian summertime favourite — and this one, sporting our national colours of red and white, is no exception.

Makes 8 servings

28	small new red potatoes (about 3 lb/1.5 kg)	28
12	radishes	12
2	stalks tender celery, sliced	2
½ cup	thinly sliced red onion	125 mL
¼ cup	chopped fresh dill	50 mL
DRESSING		
½ cup	vegetable oil	125 mL
¼ cup	lemon juice	50 mL
1 tbsp	grainy or Dijon mustard	15 mL
½ tsp	each salt and pepper	2 mL
¼ tsp	granulated sugar	1 mL

↞43

⇐ In saucepan of boiling salted water, cover and cook potatoes just until tender, 10 to 15 minutes. Drain and let cool; cut into quarters.

⇐ Meanwhile, cut radishes in half and thinly slice; place in large bowl. Add celery, onion and half of the dill. Add potatoes.

⇐ **DRESSING:** In small bowl, whisk together oil, lemon juice, mustard, salt, pepper and sugar; pour over potato mixture and gently toss to coat. *Make-ahead: Cover and refrigerate for up to 4 hours.* Serve sprinkled with remaining dill.

PER SERVING: about 276 cal, 3 g pro, 14 g total fat (1 g sat. fat), 37 g carb, 3 g fibre, 0 mg chol, 524 mg sodium % RDI: 2% calcium, 10% iron, 40% vit C, 11% folate.

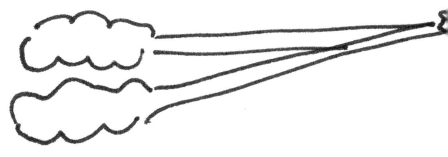

GRILLED CHICKEN SALAD

A homemade peppercorn ranch dressing is bound to taste better than a commercial one and takes just minutes to whisk in a bowl — or shake in a jar.

Makes 4 servings

1 tbsp	chopped fresh basil	**15 mL**
2 tsp	vegetable oil	**10 mL**
2 tsp	Dijon mustard	**10 mL**
¼ tsp	each salt and pepper	**1 mL**
4	boneless skinless chicken breasts	**4**
6 cups	torn mixed greens	**1.5 L**
1 cup	alfalfa sprouts	**250 mL**
1	piece (6 inches/15 cm) cucumber, sliced	**1**
½ cup	thinly sliced radishes	**125 mL**

PEPPERCORN RANCH DRESSING

½ cup	plain yogurt	**125 mL**
⅓ cup	light mayonnaise	**75 mL**
1 tsp	coarsely ground pepper	**5 mL**
½ tsp	Dijon mustard	**2 mL**
¼ tsp	granulated sugar	**1 mL**
Pinch	salt	**Pinch**

← In small bowl, stir together basil, oil, mustard, salt and pepper; brush over chicken. Place on greased grill or in grill pan or skillet over medium heat; close lid and grill, turning once, until no longer pink inside, 12 to 15 minutes. Let cool slightly; thinly slice across the grain.

← Meanwhile, in large bowl, toss together salad greens, sprouts, cucumber and radishes. Arrange chicken strips over top.

← **PEPPERCORN RANCH DRESSING:** In small bowl, whisk together yogurt, mayonnaise, pepper, mustard, sugar and salt; drizzle over salad. Toss to serve.

PER SERVING: about 291 cal, 36 g pro, 12 g total fat (2 g sat. fat), 10 g carb, 2 g fibre, 87 mg chol, 435 mg sodium. % RDI: 12% calcium, 13% iron, 20% vit A, 32% vit C, 42% folate.

GOLDEN CORN MUFFINS

Mildly spiced and with a slight cornmeal crunch, these make delicious main course partners.

Makes 12 muffins

1 cup	cornmeal	250 mL
1 cup	all-purpose flour	250 mL
1 tbsp	baking powder	15 mL
½ tsp	salt	2 mL
¼ tsp	hot pepper flakes	1 mL
1½ cups	low-fat plain yogurt	375 mL
⅓ cup	butter, melted	75 mL
2	eggs, separated	2
2 tbsp	granulated sugar	25 mL

← In large bowl, whisk together cornmeal, flour, baking powder, salt and hot pepper flakes. In separate bowl, whisk together yogurt, butter and egg yolks; pour over dry ingredients and stir just until combined.

← In another bowl, beat egg whites until soft peaks form; beat in sugar, 1 tbsp (15 mL) at a time, until stiff glossy peaks form. Fold into batter. Scrape into greased or paper-lined muffin cups.

← Bake in centre of 400°F (200°C) oven until cake tester inserted in centre comes out clean, about 18 minutes.

PER MUFFIN: about 166 cal, 5 g pro, 7 g total fat (4 g sat. fat), 21 g carb, 2 g fibre, 47 mg chol, 245 mg sodium. % RDI: 8% calcium, 5% iron, 7% vit A, 10% folate.

SALAD DRESSINGS WITH A LIGHT TOUCH

Each of these lightened-up dressings makes enough for three four-serving salads (each using 8 cups/2 L greens and/or vegetables). Refrigerate them in airtight containers for up to five days.

LEMON ORANGE POPPY SEED DRESSING

This citrusy dressing has a hint of sweetness that goes nicely with torn spinach and thinly sliced radishes.

Makes 1 cup (250 mL)

⅓ cup	light sour cream	75 mL
¼ cup	minced sweet onion	50 mL
¼ cup	light mayonnaise	50 mL
½ tsp	grated lemon rind	2 mL
2 tbsp	each lemon and orange juice	25 mL
1 tbsp	poppy seeds	15 mL
1 tsp	liquid honey	5 mL

← In small bowl, whisk together sour cream, onion, mayonnaise, lemon rind, lemon and orange juices, poppy seeds and honey.

PER 1 TBSP (15 mL): about 24 cal, 1 g pro, 2 g total fat (trace sat. fat), 2 g carb, trace fibre, 2 mg chol, 32 mg sodium. % RDI: 2% calcium, 1% iron, 3% vit C, 1% folate.

FETA CHEESE DRESSING

This creamy Greek-inspired dressing uses mainly buttermilk in order to keep the fat content as low as possible.

Makes 1 cup (250 mL)

½ cup	buttermilk or plain yogurt	125 mL
⅓ cup	crumbled feta cheese	75 mL
2 tbsp	light mayonnaise	25 mL
1 tsp	Dijon mustard	5 mL
1	small clove garlic, minced	1
½ tsp	dried oregano	2 mL
¼ tsp	pepper	1 mL

← In small bowl, whisk together buttermilk, feta cheese, mayonnaise, mustard, garlic, oregano and pepper.

PER 1 TBSP (15 mL): about 16 cal, 1 g pro, 1 g total fat (1 g sat. fat), 1 g carb, 0 g fibre, 3 mg chol, 55 mg sodium. % RDI: 2% calcium, 1% iron.

LEMON HERB DRESSING

This fresh dressing is a winner tossed with warm peas or beans or drizzled over asparagus. Honey sweetens the dressing, so you can get away with using half the oil that you would traditionally need to balance the lemon juice.

Makes 1 cup (250 mL)

¼ cup	minced fresh mint	50 mL
¼ cup	lemon juice	50 mL
¼ cup	extra-virgin olive oil	50 mL
2 tbsp	minced fresh dill	25 mL
2 tbsp	Dijon mustard	25 mL
1 tbsp	white wine vinegar	15 mL
1 tbsp	liquid honey	15 mL
1	green onion, finely chopped	1
½ tsp	each salt and pepper	2 mL

← In small bowl, whisk together mint, lemon juice, oil, dill, mustard, vinegar, honey, onion, salt and pepper.

PER 1 TBSP (15 mL): about 37 cal, trace pro, 4 g total fat (trace sat. fat), 2 g carb, 0 g fibre, 0 mg chol, 98 mg sodium. % RDI: 1% iron, 2% vit C, 1% folate.

LIGHTENED-UP GREEN GODDESS DRESSING

Use this zesty dressing as a sandwich spread or even a vegetable dip.

Makes 1 cup (250 mL)

⅓ cup	each light mayonnaise and light sour cream	75 mL
¼ cup	minced fresh parsley	50 mL
1	green onion, finely chopped	1
1	small clove garlic, minced	1
1 tbsp	tarragon vinegar or wine vinegar	15 mL
1 tbsp	Dijon mustard	15 mL
1 tsp	Worcestershire sauce	5 mL
1 tsp	anchovy paste	5 mL

← In small bowl, whisk together mayonnaise, sour cream, parsley, green onion, garlic, vinegar, mustard, Worcestershire sauce and anchovy paste.

PER 1 TBSP (15 mL): about 24 cal, 1 g pro, 2 g total fat (trace sat. fat), 1 g carb, 0 g fibre, 3 mg chol, 67 mg sodium. % RDI: 1% calcium, 1% iron, 1% vit A, 2% vit C, 1% folate.

JAPANESE COLD NOODLE "CHEF SALAD"

You can add other ingredients, such as sliced mushrooms or tofu and finely shredded red or white cabbage or carrots. Toast sesame seeds briefly in a dry skillet.

Makes 4 servings

2	eggs	2
Pinch	salt	Pinch
1 tbsp	vegetable oil	15 mL
12 oz	Chinese wheat noodles, ramen or linguini	375 g
2 tsp	sesame oil	10 mL
8 oz	ham, julienned	250 g
1	sweet red pepper, thinly sliced	1
1 cup	shredded cucumber	250 mL
4 cups	shredded iceberg lettuce	1 L
2	green onions, thinly sliced	2
4 tsp	toasted sesame seeds	20 mL
SAUCE		
⅔ cup	chicken stock	150 mL
⅓ cup	granulated sugar	75 mL
⅓ cup	rice or cider vinegar	75 mL
3 tbsp	soy sauce	50 mL
1 tbsp	grated gingerroot	15 mL

SAUCE: In saucepan, bring stock, sugar, vinegar, soy sauce and ginger to boil; reduce heat and simmer for 5 minutes. Strain and refrigerate until cool. *Make-ahead: Refrigerate in airtight container for up to 3 days.*

Beat together eggs, salt and 1 tsp (5 mL) of the vegetable oil. Heat 6-inch (15 cm) nonstick skillet over medium-high heat; brush lightly with some of the remaining vegetable oil. Pour in about one-quarter of the egg mixture, tilting pan to spread evenly; cook until top is set, about 30 seconds. Slide out onto cutting board. Repeat with remaining egg mixture to make 4 thin omelettes; stack and cut into fine shreds.

In large pot of boiling salted water, cook noodles until tender but firm, about 5 minutes; drain and chill under cold water. Drain well. In bowl, toss noodles with sesame oil.

Arrange noodles on 4 dinner plates. Attractively top with eggs, ham, red pepper, cucumber and lettuce. Sprinkle with green onions. *Make-ahead: Cover and refrigerate for up to 4 hours.* Sprinkle with sauce and sesame seeds.

PER SERVING: about 696 cal, 27 g pro, 30 g total fat (10 g sat. fat), 81 g carb, 6 g fibre, 120 mg chol, 1,986 mg sodium. % RDI: 7% calcium, 22% iron, 24% vit A, 103% vit C, 37% folate.

CAESAR SALAD WITH CRUNCHY CROUTONS

50 →

Ask a kid what their favourite salad is, and you guessed it: Caesar. This one is easy to make, and if you're in a hurry use precooked bacon bits and seasoned croutons.

Makes 4 to 6 servings

2	slices bacon	**2**
Half	head romaine lettuce	**Half**
2 tbsp	grated Parmesan cheese	**25 mL**
CROUTONS		
1 tbsp	extra-virgin olive oil	**15 mL**
2	slices (½ inch/1 cm thick) crusty bread	**2**
DRESSING		
2 tbsp	extra-virgin olive oil	**25 mL**
2 tbsp	light mayonnaise	**25 mL**
1 tbsp	grated Parmesan cheese	**15 mL**
1½ tsp	white wine vinegar	**7 mL**
1 tsp	each Dijon mustard and anchovy paste	**5 mL**
1	clove garlic, minced	**1**
¼ tsp	pepper and Worcestershire sauce	**1 mL**

← **CROUTONS:** Brush oil over both sides of bread; cut into ½-inch (1 cm) cubes. Bake on rimmed baking sheet in 350°F (180°C) oven, stirring once, until golden and crisp, 15 to 18 minutes. Let cool. *Make-ahead: Store in airtight container for up to 1 week.*

← **DRESSING:** In bowl, whisk together oil, mayonnaise, cheese, vinegar, mustard, anchovy paste, garlic, pepper and Worcestershire sauce. *Make-ahead: Cover and refrigerate for up to 24 hours.*

← In nonstick skillet, cook bacon over medium heat until crispy, about 4 minutes. Let cool on paper towels; crumble.

← Meanwhile, tear lettuce into bite-size pieces to make about 10 cups (2.5 L); place in large bowl. Add bacon, cheese, croutons and dressing; toss to combine.

PER EACH OF 6 SERVINGS: about 132 cal, 4 g pro, 11 g total fat (2 g sat. fat), 6 g carb, 1 g fibre, 5 mg chol, 213 mg sodium.

% RDI: 6% calcium, 6% iron, 10% vit A, 15% vit C, 26% folate.

THAI MANGO SALAD

The traditional Thai salad is sweet and spicy, with finely chopped pork, dried shrimp, peanuts and chilies. Here we've skipped the meat and seafood and mixed the traditional with a few creative ideas of our own.

Makes 6 servings

½ cup	coarsely chopped peanuts	125 mL
2	firm mangoes (about 2 lb/1 kg total)	2
1	sweet red pepper	1
2	carrots, coarsely grated	2
4 cups	torn mixed greens	1 L
¼ cup	thinly sliced green onions	50 mL
2 tbsp	coarsely chopped fresh mint	25 mL
DRESSING		
¼ cup	vegetable oil	50 mL
1 tsp	grated lime rind	5 mL
2 tbsp	lime juice	25 mL
1 tbsp	fish sauce or soy sauce	15 mL
2 tsp	granulated sugar	10 mL
1 tsp	minced hot pepper (or ¼ tsp/1 mL hot pepper sauce)	5 mL
¼ tsp	each salt and pepper	1 mL

◆ In skillet, toast peanuts over medium heat until fragrant and dark golden, about 8 minutes. Set aside.

◆ Peel, pit and thinly slice mangoes lengthwise. Seed, core and thinly slice red pepper. Set aside.

◆ **DRESSING:** In large bowl, whisk together oil, lime rind and juice, fish sauce, sugar, hot pepper, salt and pepper. Add mangoes, red pepper, carrots, mixed greens, green onions and mint; toss to coat. Serve sprinkled with peanuts.

PER SERVING: about 251 cal, 5 g pro, 15 g total fat (2 g sat. fat), 28 g carb, 5 g fibre, 0 mg chol, 403 mg sodium % RDI: 6% calcium, 8% iron, 136% vit A, 128% vit C, 34% folate.

ROASTED ROOTS SALAD

Roasting caramelizes root vegetables, releasing their natural sweetness that balances a piquant balsamic dressing.

Makes 6 servings

1	head garlic	**1**
4	beets (about 1 lb/500 g)	**4**
4	carrots (or half rutabaga), about 1 lb (500 g)	**4**
2	sweet potatoes (about 1 lb/500 g)	**2**
1	celery root (or 4 potatoes), about 1 lb (500 g)	**1**
3 tbsp	extra-virgin olive oil	**50 mL**
½ tsp	each salt and pepper	**2 mL**

DRESSING

¼ cup	chopped fresh mint (or 1 tsp/5 mL dried)	**50 mL**
2 tbsp	extra-virgin olive oil	**25 mL**
2 tbsp	balsamic vinegar	**25 mL**
¼ tsp	salt	**1 mL**

←55 Trim tip off garlic. Peel and cut beets, carrots, sweet potatoes and celery root into 1-inch (2.5 cm) cubes.

← In large bowl, toss garlic and vegetables with oil, salt and pepper to coat. Spread on large greased or foil-lined rimmed baking sheet; roast in 425°F (220°C) oven, stirring once, until tender and potatoes are golden, 45 to 55 minutes.

← **DRESSING:** Squeeze garlic pulp into large salad bowl. Add mint, oil, vinegar and salt; mash together. Add roasted vegetables; toss to coat. Serve hot or warm.

PER SERVING: about 247 cal, 4 g pro, 12 g total fat (2 g sat. fat), 34 g carb, 6 g fibre, 0 mg chol, 440 mg sodium. % RDI: 3% calcium, 13% iron, 272% vit A, 37% vit C, 33% folate.

SPINACH RADICCHIO SALAD WITH HONEY MUSTARD DRESSING

If your salads tend to be the same old lettuce and veggies, try this colourful combo. It's a salad that will win raves from the kids who can't resist cashews, and company will love it, too.

Makes 4 servings

6 cups	spinach leaves	**1.5 L**
2 cups	torn radicchio leaves	**500 mL**
1 cup	thinly sliced mushrooms	**250 mL**
⅓ cup	cashews, halved or chopped	**75 mL**
HONEY MUSTARD DRESSING		
3 tbsp	extra-virgin olive oil	**50 mL**
2 tbsp	wine vinegar	**25 mL**
1	clove garlic, minced	**1**
1½ tsp	Dijon mustard	**7 mL**
½ tsp	liquid honey	**2 mL**
¼ tsp	each salt and pepper	**1 mL**

← **HONEY MUSTARD DRESSING:** In salad bowl, whisk together oil, vinegar, garlic, mustard, honey, salt and pepper; set aside.

← Trim stems from spinach; tear leaves into bite-size pieces and add to bowl. Add radicchio and mushrooms; toss to coat. Sprinkle with cashews.

PER SERVING: about 186 cal, 5 g pro, 16 g total fat (2 g sat. fat), 9 g carb, 3 g fibre, 0 mg chol, 242 mg sodium. % RDI: 9% calcium, 23% iron, 57% vit A, 43% vit C, 84% folate.

VARIATION

SPINACH RADICCHIO SALAD WITH SESAME DRESSING

Omit Honey Mustard Dressing and cashews. In salad bowl, whisk together 3 tbsp (50 mL) vegetable oil, 2 tbsp (25 mL) rice wine vinegar, 1 tbsp (15 mL) sesame oil, 1 tbsp (15 mL) soy sauce, 1 tsp (5 mL) Dijon mustard and ½ tsp (2 mL) granulated sugar. Toss with salad. Sprinkle with sesame seeds.

SPICED CARROT SALAD

Carrots are a terrific salad ingredient — inexpensive even in the depths of winter. They taste wonderful with this simple Morrocan-inspired dressing.

Makes 4 to 6 servings

14	carrots (about 2 lb/1 kg)	14
1 tbsp	extra-virgin olive oil	15 mL
2	shallots (or 1 small onion), finely chopped	2
2	cloves garlic, minced	2
½ tsp	each salt, ground cumin, cinnamon and paprika	2 mL
Pinch	cayenne pepper	Pinch
2 tbsp	lemon juice	25 mL
¼ cup	chopped fresh coriander	50 mL

← Diagonally cut carrots into ½-inch (1 cm) thick slices. In large pot of boiling salted water, cover and cook carrots until tender-crisp, about 5 minutes. Chill under cold water; drain.

← Meanwhile, in large skillet, heat oil over medium heat; fry shallots and garlic, stirring occasionally, until softened, about 3 minutes.

← Stir in salt, cumin, cinnamon, paprika and cayenne pepper; fry until fragrant, about 1 minute. Add carrots and lemon juice; toss to coat. Pour into salad bowl; stir in coriander.

PER EACH OF 6 SERVINGS: about 97 cal, 2 g pro, 3 g total fat (trace sat. fat), 18 g carb, 4 g fibre, 0 mg chol, 662 mg sodium. % RDI: 5% calcium, 9% iron, 383% vit A, 8% vit C, 10% folate.

←59

CHAPTER 3

SANDW
AND
WRAPS

ICHES

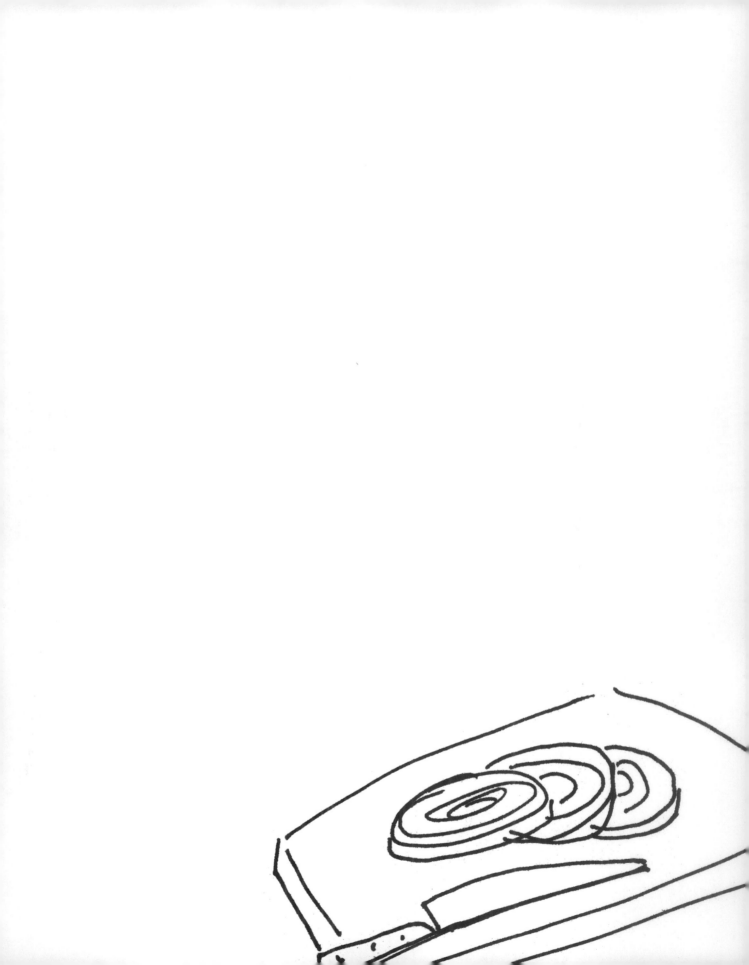

PIZZA PANINI

When popular pizza flavours team up in a crusty toasted sandwich, it's guaranteed to be the most requested. Toast in a panini or sandwich maker, if you have this handy small appliance, or follow our easy outdoor/indoor grilling instructions.

Makes 2 servings

2	oval panini buns	2
¼ cup	pizza or pasta sauce	50 mL
FILLING		
2 oz	thinly sliced pepperoni or salami	60 g
½ cup	thinly sliced sweet green pepper	125 mL
¼ cup	sliced black or green olives (optional)	50 mL
⅓ cup	shredded part-skim mozzarella cheese	75 mL

← Cut buns horizontally in half; spread cut sides with pizza sauce.

← **FILLING:** Layer pepperoni, green pepper, and olives (if using) on bottom halves; sprinkle with cheese. Sandwich with top halves, cut side down.

← Place on grill or in grill pan or skillet over medium-low heat; close lid and grill, pressing panini occasionally with spatula and rotating one-quarter turn halfway through to create crosshatched grill marks, until bottom is crusty, about 4 minutes.

← Turn and grill, pressing and rotating halfway through, until crusty and cheese is melted, about 4 minutes.

PER SERVING: about 402 cal, 18 g pro, 19 g total fat (7 g sat. fat), 39 g carb, 2 g fibre, 33 mg chol, 1,201 mg sodium. % RDI: 19% calcium, 20% iron, 10% vit A, 28% vit C, 26% folate.

← 67

VARIATIONS

HAM, CHUTNEY AND CHEESE PANINI

Substitute 2 tbsp (25 mL) mango or other fruit chutney and 1 tbsp (15 mL) Dijon mustard for the pizza sauce.

← **FILLING:** Substitute 2 oz (60 g) shaved Black Forest ham, ¼ cup (50 mL) thinly sliced sweet onion and ⅓ cup (75 mL) shredded Gruyère or 2 oz (60 g) thinly sliced Brie cheese.

ARUGULA AND PROSCIUTTO PANINI

Substitute ¼ cup (50 mL) softened herbed goat cheese or herbed cream cheese for the pizza sauce.

← **FILLING:** Substitute 2 oz (60 g) sliced prosciutto and ⅔ cup (150 mL) lightly packed arugula or spinach leaves.

SANTA FE BEEF FAJITAS

Fajitas, today's delicious and nutritious fast food, roll up a variety of family-pleasing fillings in just 15 minutes.

Makes 4 servings

2 tsp	vegetable oil	10 mL
1 lb	lean ground beef	500 g
¼ tsp	each salt and pepper	1 mL
2 tbsp	chopped fresh herbs (such as coriander or parsley)	25 mL
4	large flour tortillas, warmed	4

VEGETABLES

1	sweet red pepper, sliced	1
Half	red onion, sliced	Half
½ cup	corn kernels	125 mL
1	clove garlic, minced	1

FLAVOURING

½ cup	barbecue sauce	125 mL
1 tbsp	chopped fresh or pickled jalapeño pepper	15 mL
1 tsp	chili powder	5 mL

← In large nonstick skillet, heat oil over medium-high heat; stir-fry beef until browned, about 5 minutes. With slotted spoon, transfer beef to plate. Drain any fat from pan.

← **VEGETABLES:** Add red pepper, onion, corn, garlic, salt and pepper to pan; stir-fry until softened, about 5 minutes.

← **FLAVOURING:** Add barbecue sauce, jalapeño pepper and chili powder; cook over medium heat, stirring, for 2 minutes. Return beef and any accumulated juices to pan; cook for 1 minute. Sprinkle with herbs.

← Cut tortillas in half. Mound about ½ cup (125 mL) filling on each; roll up sides to form cone. Secure bottom with waxed paper or long toothpicks.

PER SERVING: about 454 cal, 29 g pro, 17 g total fat (6 g sat. fat), 45 g carb, 4 g fibre, 60 mg chol, 748 mg sodium. % RDI: 5% calcium, 34% iron, 19% vit A, 98% vit C, 40% folate.

VARIATIONS

CREOLE CATFISH FAJITAS

Substitute 1 lb (500 g) catfish or tilapia fillets, cut in ½-inch (1 cm) wide strips, for the beef.

← **VEGETABLES:** Substitute 1 each sweet green pepper and onion, sliced, ½ cup (125 mL) chopped celery and 2 cloves garlic, minced.

← **FLAVOURING:** Substitute ½ cup (125 mL) ketchup, 1 tbsp (15 mL) Cajun seasoning, and ¼ tsp (1 mL) cayenne pepper (optional).

SPICY SAUSAGE FAJITAS

Substitute 1 lb (500 g) hot or mild Italian sausages, casings removed, for the beef.

← **VEGETABLES:** Substitute 1 each sweet green pepper, carrot and onion, sliced, and 2 cloves garlic, minced.

← **FLAVOURING:** Substitute ¾ cup (175 mL) hot or mild salsa, 1 tomato, chopped, 1 jalapeño pepper, seeded and chopped, and pinch cayenne pepper (optional).

REUBEN SANDWICHES

This classic sandwich of meat, cheese and sauerkraut makes a hearty meal.

Makes 4 servings

1½ cups	sauerkraut	375 mL
2 tsp	butter	10 mL
1	small onion, chopped	1
¼ tsp	pepper	1 mL
¼ cup	light mayonnaise	50 mL
¼ cup	sweet relish	50 mL
2 tbsp	ketchup	25 mL
8	slices pumpernickel bread	8
12 oz	shaved pastrami	375 g
4	slices Swiss cheese	4

← Rinse and drain sauerkraut. In nonstick skillet, melt butter over medium heat; cook sauerkraut, onion and pepper for 4 minutes.

← In bowl, stir together mayonnaise, relish and ketchup; spread over bread. Divide sauerkraut mixture, pastrami and cheese evenly over half of the bread slices. Top with remaining bread; press lightly.

← Place sandwiches on rimmed baking sheet. Broil, about 6 inches (15 cm) from heat, turning once, until cheese melts, about 5 minutes.

PER SERVING: about 670 cal, 29 g pro, 41 g total fat (16 g sat. fat), 46 g carb, 7 g fibre, 110 mg chol, 2,346 mg sodium. % RDI: 32% calcium, 34% iron, 10% vit A, 23% vit C, 20% folate.

BUTTON MUSHROOM SALAD

Mushroom lovers will find this tasty salad a great side for the sandwich and a delicious item for a buffet table.

←71

Makes 4 servings

4 cups	halved button mushrooms (about 12 oz/375 g)	1 L
1 cup	chopped sweet red pepper	250 mL
4	green onions, sliced	4
3 tbsp	balsamic vinegar	50 mL
2 tbsp	chopped fresh parsley	25 mL
2 tbsp	extra-virgin olive oil	25 mL
½ tsp	each salt and pepper	2 mL
4	large lettuce leaves	4

← In large bowl, gently toss together mushrooms, red pepper, onions, vinegar, parsley, oil, salt and pepper. Serve in lettuce leaves.

PER SERVING: about 107 cal, 2 g pro, 7 g total fat (1 g sat. fat), 10 g carb, 2 g fibre, 0 mg chol, 234 mg sodium. % RDI: 3% calcium, 11% iron, 25% vit A, 132% vit C, 19% folate

CHICKEN COUSCOUS WRAPS WITH RED PEPPER MAYONNAISE

In the summer, prepare the couscous and the roasted pepper mayonnaise in the kitchen, then head outside to the barbecue. When it's too cold, grill the chicken on an indoor grill or grill pan.

Makes 4 servings

½ tsp	salt	2 mL
⅓ cup	whole wheat couscous	75 mL
¼ cup	minced fresh parsley	50 mL
2	boneless skinless chicken breasts	2
¼ tsp	pepper	1 mL
2	small zucchini	2
1 tsp	extra-virgin olive oil	5 mL
4	large whole wheat flour tortillas	4
1 cup	alfalfa sprouts	250 mL
RED PEPPER MAYONNAISE		
⅓ cup	chopped roasted red pepper	75 mL
¼ cup	light mayonnaise	50 mL
1	clove garlic, minced	1
Pinch	cayenne pepper	Pinch

← 73

← In saucepan, bring ½ cup (125 mL) water and pinch of the salt to boil. Remove from heat and stir in couscous; cover and let stand for 5 minutes. Fluff with fork. Stir in parsley.

← **RED PEPPER MAYONNAISE:** Meanwhile, in food processor, whirl red pepper with mayonnaise until smooth; stir in garlic and cayenne pepper. Set aside.

← Sprinkle chicken with pepper and half of the remaining salt. Place on greased grill over medium-high heat; close lid and grill, turning once, until no longer pink inside, about 12 minutes. Remove to cutting board; cut into ¼-inch (5 mm) thick slices.

← Meanwhile, diagonally cut zucchini into ¼-inch (5 mm) thick slices; brush with oil and sprinkle with remaining salt. Grill over medium-high heat, turning once, until translucent and grill-marked, about 4 minutes.

← Cut tortillas in half; spread each half with Red Pepper Mayonnaise. Layer couscous, chicken, zucchini and sprouts down centre. Roll up sides to form cone; secure bottom with waxed paper or long toothpicks.

PER SERVING: about 344 cal, 27 g pro, 8 g total fat (1 g sat. fat), 50 g carb, 7 g fibre, 55 mg chol, 749 mg sodium. % RDI: 4% calcium, 19% iron, 8% vit A, 45% vit C, 16% folate.

SAUCY BEEF AND MUSHROOM SANDWICHES

In the old days, serving sandwiches as supper was a sign of bad planning. How times have changed!

Makes 4 servings

12 oz	top sirloin grilling steak	375 g
1 tbsp	vegetable oil	15 mL
1	onion, sliced	1
2 cups	sliced mushrooms	500 mL
¼ tsp	each salt and pepper	1 mL
½ cup	barbecue sauce	125 mL
2 tbsp	tomato paste	25 mL
½ tsp	Worcestershire sauce	2 mL
Dash	hot pepper sauce	Dash
4	whole wheat kaiser rolls, halved and toasted	4

← 75

← Cut beef into ¼-inch (5 mm) thick strips. In large nonstick skillet, heat oil over medium-high heat; stir-fry beef until browned but still pink inside, about 2 minutes. Transfer to plate.

← Drain any fat from pan. Add onion, mushrooms, salt and pepper; fry, stirring occasionally, until mushroom liquid is evaporated, about 4 minutes.

← Add barbecue sauce, tomato paste, Worcestershire sauce and hot pepper sauce. Return beef and any accumulated juices to pan; toss to coat and heat through. Sandwich in buns.

PER SERVING: about 351 cal, 25 g pro, 10 g total fat (2 g sat. fat), 41 g carb, 6 g fibre, 40 mg chol, 763 mg sodium. % RDI: 9% calcium, 31% iron, 5% vit A, 13% vit C, 14% folate.

GARLIC RAPINI AND SAUSAGE SANDWICHES

This combo of edgy rapini and crisp juicy sausage is just a tad daring — but addictive. You'll love it!

Makes 4 servings

4	hot or sweet Italian sausages	4
4	whole wheat panini buns	4
2 tbsp	each light mayonnaise and Dijon mustard	25 mL
4	slices provolone cheese	4
GARLIC RAPINI		
1	bunch rapini (about 1 lb/500 g)	1
3 tbsp	extra-virgin olive oil	50 mL
4	cloves garlic, minced	4
Pinch	hot pepper flakes	Pinch
¼ tsp	salt	1 mL

← Cut sausages in half lengthwise. In nonstick skillet, fry sausages over medium-high heat, turning occasionally, until crusty, brown and no longer pink inside, about 8 minutes. Cut into bite-size pieces if desired.

← **GARLIC RAPINI:** Meanwhile, trim bases of rapini stalks. In large deep skillet of boiling water, cover and cook rapini until stalks are tender, about 6 minutes. Drain and chill under cold water; drain and pat dry. Chop coarsely; set aside.

← In same skillet, heat oil over medium heat; cook garlic and hot pepper flakes until garlic begins to brown, about 2 minutes. Add rapini and salt; sauté until hot.

← Cut buns in half; spread cut side of bottoms with mayonnaise and mustard. Top with rapini, sausages and cheese. Broil, along with top halves cut side up, until cheese melts, about 2 minutes.

PER SERVING: about 616 cal, 32 g pro, 38 g total fat (12 g sat. fat), 40 g carb, 7 g fibre, 64 mg chol, 1,493 mg sodium. % RDI: 51% calcium, 34% iron, 39% vit A, 57% vit C, 15% folate.

CURRIED CHICKEN SALAD MINI-PITAS

Curry and petite pitas give a nouveau twist to party sandwiches. You can vary the fillings, stuffing the pitas with ever-popular salmon, tuna or egg salad. Of course, you can use the filling to stuff large pitas or rolls as well.

Makes 24 pieces

2	cooked boneless skinless chicken breasts	2
⅓ cup	diced sweet red pepper	75 mL
⅓ cup	diced celery	75 mL
2	green onions, thinly sliced	2
1	apple	1
24	mini-pitas	24
	Leaf lettuce	

DRESSING

⅓ cup	light mayonnaise	75 mL
3 tbsp	chopped fresh coriander	50 mL
1 tsp	lemon juice	5 mL
½ tsp	minced gingerroot	2 mL
½ tsp	mild curry paste	2 mL
¼ tsp	each ground cumin and salt	1 mL
Pinch	pepper	Pinch

← 79

← In large bowl and using fingers, shred chicken finely to make 2 cups (500 mL); add red pepper, celery and onions.

← **DRESSING:** In small bowl, stir together mayonnaise, coriander, lemon juice, ginger, curry paste, cumin, salt and pepper; add to chicken mixture and stir to combine. *Make-ahead: Cover and refrigerate for up to 24 hours.*

← Halve and core apple; cut each half into 12 slices. Cut top third off each pita; open and place inverted piece in bottom as reinforcement. Line with lettuce; spoon in chicken salad and top with apple slice.

PER PIECE: about 50 cal, 3 g pro, 1 g total fat (trace sat. fat), 6 g carb, trace fibre, 7 mg chol, 96 mg sodium. % RDI: 1% calcium, 2% iron, 1% vit A, 5% vit C, 5% folate.

TIP

Use leftover cooked or deli rotisserie chicken. Or poach the breasts in skillet of lightly salted simmering water until no longer pink inside, about 10 minutes.

CORNMEAL-CRUSTED RAINBOW TROUT SANDWICHES

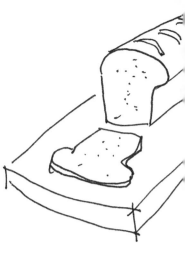

Somehow we couldn't make this crusty sandwich without tomato and lettuce — that BLT tug of tradition!

Makes 4 servings

8	slices bacon	8
4	skinless rainbow trout fillets (1 lb/500 g)	4
¼ tsp	each salt and pepper	1 mL
⅓ cup	cornmeal	75 mL
1 tbsp	vegetable oil	15 mL
4	oval buns, halved	4
TARTAR SAUCE		
⅓ cup	light mayonnaise	75 mL
2 tbsp	sweet green relish	25 mL
1 tbsp	chopped rinsed drained capers	15 mL
1 tsp	lemon juice	5 mL
Pinch	each salt and pepper	Pinch

← **TARTAR SAUCE:** In small bowl, mix together mayonnaise, relish, capers, lemon juice, salt and pepper; set aside. *Make-ahead: Cover and refrigerate for up to 24 hours.*

← Cut bacon in half crosswise. In nonstick skillet, fry bacon over medium-high heat, turning once, until crisp, about 6 minutes. Transfer to paper towel–lined plate to drain. Drain fat from pan; wipe clean.

← Meanwhile, sprinkle fish with salt and pepper. Sprinkle cornmeal in shallow dish; press fish into cornmeal, turning to coat.

← In same skillet, heat oil over medium heat; fry fish, turning once, until crisp, golden and flakes easily when tested, 6 to 8 minutes.

← Meanwhile, in toaster oven, toast cut sides of buns until golden, about 1 minute. Sandwich fish in buns along with Tartar Sauce and bacon.

PER SERVING: about 529 cal, 32 g pro, 25 g total fat (6 g sat. fat), 42 g carb, 2 g fibre 77 mg chol, 969 mg sodium. % RDI: 13% calcium, 20% iron, 8% vit A, 5% vit C, 34% folate.

TUNA PAN BAGNAT

82 →

Pan bagnat, a layered pepper, tomato, tuna and olive sandwich, is a mainstay in southern France, and seems right at home in Canadian kitchens.

Makes 4 servings

1	baguette	1
3 tbsp	extra-virgin olive oil	50 mL
1 tbsp	red wine vinegar	15 mL
2 tsp	anchovy paste (optional)	10 mL
¼ tsp	each salt and pepper	1 mL
½ cup	sliced sweet green pepper	125 mL
¼ cup	sliced black olives (preferably oil-cured)	50 mL
¼ cup	finely chopped red onion	50 mL
1	small tomato, sliced	1
2 tbsp	drained capers	25 mL
1	can (170 g) solid white tuna, drained and broken into chunks	1

← Cut bread in half horizontally without cutting all the way through.

← In small bowl, whisk together oil, vinegar, anchovy paste (if using), salt and pepper; brush half over cut surfaces of loaf.

← Arrange green pepper, olives, onion, tomato, capers and tuna on bottom half of loaf; drizzle with remaining dressing. Close top of loaf over filling.

Make-ahead: Wrap in plastic wrap and refrigerate for up to 24 hours.

PER SERVING: about 363 cal, 16 g pro, 14 g total fat (2 g sat. fat), 43 g carb, 3 g fibre, 14 mg chol, 872 mg sodium. % RDI: 6% calcium, 19% iron, 4% vit A, 27% vit C, 37% folate.

TIP

It is traditional to use an oil-packed tuna in pan bagnat, however, water-packed is lower in fat and thus is a lighter choice.

ALL-DAY-BREAKFAST IN A BUN

Here's one more way to savour that irresistible bacon-and-egg combo — delicious and satisfying morning, noon or night. The eggs are cooked as an omelette and tucked into a toasted bun along with cheese, tomato, lettuce and, naturally, bacon. Greens with Honey Lime Dressing is the perfect accompaniment.

Makes 4 servings

1 tbsp	butter	**15 mL**
8	slices peameal or back bacon	**8**
6	eggs	**6**
¼ cup	milk	**50 mL**
2	green onions, thinly sliced	**2**
¼ tsp	each salt and pepper	**1 mL**
4	thin slices Havarti or Cheddar cheese	**4**
8	thin slices tomato	**8**
4	leaves leaf lettuce (optional)	**4**
4	whole wheat kaiser or flat buns, halved and toasted	**4**

← In large nonstick skillet, melt 1 tsp (5 mL) of the butter over medium heat; brown bacon, about 4 minutes. Remove to plate and keep warm.

← Meanwhile, in bowl, whisk together eggs, milk, green onions, salt and pepper. In same skillet, melt remaining butter over medium heat; pour in egg mixture and cook, lifting edges with spatula to allow uncooked eggs to flow underneath, until set, about 8 minutes. Cut into quarters.

← Sandwich 2 slices bacon, 1 slice cheese, omelette quarter, 2 slices tomato, and lettuce (if using) in each bun.

PER SERVING: about 543 cal, 44 g pro, 25 g total fat (9 g sat. fat), 37 g carb, 5 g fibre, 360 mg chol, 2,324 mg sodium. % RDI: 16% calcium, 26% iron, 20% vit A, 12% vit C, 30% folate.

GREENS WITH HONEY LIME DRESSING

← 85

With just a whisk and a toss, this refreshing salad is on the table in minutes.

Makes 4 servings

¼ cup	lime juice	50 mL
3 tbsp	vegetable oil	50 mL
2 tbsp	liquid honey	25 mL
1	clove garlic, minced	1
¼ tsp	each salt and pepper	1 mL
6 cups	torn mixed greens	1.5 L

← In salad bowl, whisk together lime juice, oil, honey, garlic, salt and pepper. Add greens; toss to coat.

PER SERVING: about 140 cal, 1 g pro, 10 g total fat (1 g sat. fat), 12 g carb, 1 g fibre, 0 mg chol, 167 mg sodium. % RDI: 5% calcium, 5% iron, 18% vit A, 22% vit C, 32% folate.

HAM AND CHEESE BAGUETTE TOAST

Part French toast, part melt, these sandwiches are quick, easy and utterly pleasing.

Makes 4 servings

3	eggs	3
¼ cup	milk	50 mL
½ tsp	dried basil	2 mL
¼ tsp	each salt and pepper	1 mL
12	diagonal slices (1 inch/2.5 cm thick) baguette	12
1 tbsp	butter	15 mL
4 oz	shaved Black Forest ham	125 g
½ cup	shaved Parmesan or shredded Swiss cheese	125 mL

↞ In shallow dish, whisk together eggs, milk, basil, salt and pepper; dip bread into egg mixture to soak well.

↞ In large nonstick skillet, melt half of the butter over medium heat; fry half of the bread, turning once, until puffed and golden, about 5 minutes. Repeat with remaining butter and bread. Arrange on rimmed baking sheet.

↞ Divide ham over bread; top with cheese. Broil until bubbly and melted, about 2 minutes.

PER SERVING: about 310 cal, 20 g pro, 13 g total fat (6 g sat. fat), 26 g carb, 1 g fibre, 173 mg chol, 1,148 mg sodium. % RDI: 23% calcium, 14% iron, 12% vit A, 25% folate.

MIXED GREENS WITH SUN-DRIED TOMATO VINAIGRETTE

Sun-dried tomatoes add a depth of summer flavour to any salad dressing.

↞ 87

Makes 4 servings

2 tbsp	sun-dried tomato pesto or finely diced oil-packed sun-dried tomatoes	25 mL
2 tbsp	extra-virgin olive oil	25 mL
¼ tsp	pepper	1 mL
4 cups	torn lettuce	1 L
2	stalks celery heart, thinly sliced	2
1	small carrot, thinly sliced	1

↞ In salad bowl, whisk together tomato pesto, oil and pepper. Add lettuce, celery heart and carrot; toss to coat.

PER SERVING: about 80 cal, 1 g pro, 7 g total fat (1 g sat. fat), 4 g carb, 1 g fibre, 0 mg chol, 32 mg sodium. % RDI: 2% calcium, 4% iron, 38% vit A, 12% vit C, 18% folate.

PORTOBELLO BURGER MELTS

88 → Mushroom burgers dressed with all the tried-and-true toppings are so irresistible that they please meat-lovers, too. If you're looking for a vegetarian version, skip the Worcestershire sauce.

Makes 4 servings

2 tbsp	extra-virgin olive oil	**25 mL**
2 tbsp	balsamic vinegar	**25 mL**
1 tbsp	Dijon mustard	**15 mL**
2	cloves garlic, minced	**2**
½ tsp	Worcestershire sauce (optional)	**2 mL**
Pinch	each salt and pepper	**Pinch**
4	large portobello mushrooms (1 lb/500 g), stemmed	**4**
4	kaiser rolls or hamburger buns	**4**
¼ cup	light mayonnaise	**50 mL**
4	slices tomato	**4**
1 cup	shredded old Cheddar or Monterey Jack cheese	**250 mL**

◀ In small bowl, whisk together oil, vinegar, mustard, garlic, Worcestershire sauce (if using), salt and pepper. Brush over tops and bottoms of mushrooms; let stand for 10 minutes.

◀ Place mushrooms on greased grill, in grill pan or in skillet over medium-high heat; close lid and grill, turning once, until browned and tender, about 10 minutes.

◀ Meanwhile, cut rolls in half horizontally. Spread bottom halves with mayonnaise; top each with tomato slice and mushroom. Sprinkle with cheese; top with remaining halves of rolls. Grill, turning once, until rolls are crisp and cheese melts, about 2 minutes.

PER SERVING: about 438 cal, 15 g pro, 24 g total fat (8 g sat. fat), 42 g carb, 5 g fibre, 30 mg chol, 668 mg sodium. % RDI: 25% calcium, 25% iron, 10% vit A, 15% vit C, 35% folate.

TIP

Don't throw away the mushroom stems; chop and use them to make a flavourful cream of mushroom soup or omelette filling.

PESTO ONION STEAK SANDWICHES

An indoor electric grill or grill pan turns these summer-fresh steak sandwiches into a year-round dinner staple. If the grill is too small for both the steak and pesto onion topping, you can sautée the pesto mixture in a skillet.

Makes 4 servings

¼ cup	Dijon mustard	50 mL
¼ cup	thick teriyaki sauce	50 mL
3	cloves garlic, minced	3
¼ tsp	each salt and pepper	1 mL
1 lb	flank marinating steak	500 g
4	torpedo buns, halved	4
1	tomato, sliced	1
4	lettuce leaves	4

PESTO ONION PACKET

2 tbsp	prepared pesto	25 mL
1 tbsp	extra-virgin olive oil	15 mL
2	cloves garlic, minced	2
¼ tsp	each salt and pepper	1 mL
1	large red onion, thinly sliced	1

⬅ In shallow glass dish, whisk together mustard, teriyaki sauce, garlic, salt and pepper; remove half and set aside. Add steak to dish, turning to coat; let stand for 10 minutes. *Make-ahead: Cover and refrigerate for up to 24 hours, turning occasionally.*

⬅ Place steak on greased grill over medium-high heat; close lid and grill until rare, about 5 minutes per side, or until desired doneness. Transfer to cutting board and tent with foil; let stand for 5 minutes before slicing thinly across the grain.

⬅ **PESTO ONION PACKET:** Meanwhile, in bowl, mix together pesto, oil, garlic, salt and pepper; add onion and toss to coat. Place on large piece of heavy-duty foil; seal to form packet. Add to grill; cook until softened, about 10 minutes.

⬅ Spread reserved mustard mixture over cut sides of buns. Sandwich steak, onion mixture, tomato and lettuce in buns.

PER SERVING: about 619 cal, 39 g pro, 22 g total fat (7 g sat. fat), 66 g carb, 4 g fibre, 49 mg chol, 1,876 mg sodium. % RDI: 20% calcium, 45% iron, 4% vit A, 22% vit C, 62% folate.

SQUASH AND PEPPER BURRITOS

92 →

Here's a vegetarian meal you can bake and serve right away. The burritos also make a dandy lunch, or you can wrap them in heavy-duty foil and freeze.

Makes 4 servings

1 tbsp	vegetable oil	15 mL
1	onion, chopped	1
½ tsp	chili powder	2 mL
¼ tsp	salt	1 mL
3 cups	diced peeled butternut squash	750 mL
1	sweet green pepper, chopped	1
¼ cup	orange juice	50 mL
1	tomato, chopped	1
4	large flour tortillas	4
1 cup	shredded Cheddar or Monterey Jack cheese	250 mL

← In large nonstick skillet, heat oil over medium heat; fry onion, chili powder and salt, stirring occasionally, until softened, about 3 minutes.

← Add squash, green pepper and orange juice; cover and simmer until tender and liquid is evaporated, about 10 minutes. Stir in tomato.

← Spoon about 1 cup (250 mL) along centre of each tortilla; sprinkle with ¼ cup (50 mL) cheese. Fold up bottom edge, then sides; roll up. Place, seam side down, on greased rimmed baking sheet; bake in 350°F (180°C) oven until crispy, about 10 minutes. Cut diagonally in half.

PER SERVING: about 407 cal, 14 g pro, 17 g total fat (7 g sat. fat), 52 g carb, 5 g fibre, 30 mg chol, 669 mg sodium. % RDI: 26% calcium, 23% iron, 96% vit A, 82% vit C, 50% folate.

LEAFY AVOCADO RADISH SALAD

Avocados arrive in Canada hard as rocks. But give them three to four days at room temperature to soften and add their luxurious smoothness to a quick salad toss.

Makes 4 servings

2 tbsp	extra-virgin olive oil	25 mL
1 tbsp	grated lime or lemon rind	15 mL
2 tbsp	lime or lemon juice	25 mL
¼ tsp	each salt and pepper	1 mL
6 cups	chopped leaf lettuce	1.5 L
1	avocado, peeled and cubed	1
⅓ cup	each grated radish and sliced red onion	75 mL

← In salad bowl, whisk together oil, lime rind and juice, salt and pepper. Add lettuce, avocado, radish and onion; toss to coat.

PER SERVING: about 164 cal, 2 g pro, 15 g total fat (2 g sat. fat), 9 g carb, 4 g fibre, 0 mg chol, 159 mg sodium. % RDI: 6% calcium, 13% iron, 19% vit A, 43% vit C, 35% folate.

← 97

CHAPTER 4
PASTA

BAKED MACARONI AND BEEF

This casserole is a really robust Italian-style macaroni and cheese. It's a perfect dish for young cooks to make for their friends or family.

Makes 4 to 6 servings

1 lb	lean ground beef	500 g
1	onion, chopped	1
1	clove garlic, minced	1
1	sweet green pepper, diced	1
½ tsp	dried oregano	2 mL
1	jar (700 mL) pasta sauce	1
2 tbsp	tomato paste	25 mL
1½ cups	macaroni or ditali	375 mL
1 cup	2% cottage cheese	250 mL
½ cup	shredded provolone or part-skim mozzarella cheese	125 mL

←101

← In large nonstick skillet, fry beef over medium-high heat, breaking up with spoon, until no longer pink, about 5 minutes. Drain off any fat.

← Add onion, garlic, green pepper and oregano; fry over medium heat, stirring occasionally, until onion is softened, about 5 minutes.

← Add pasta sauce and tomato paste; bring to boil. Reduce heat to medium-low; simmer, stirring occasionally, until thick enough to mound on spoon, about 20 minutes.

← Meanwhile, in large pot of boiling salted water, cook macaroni until tender but firm, about 8 minutes; drain well.

← Spread half of the macaroni in 8-inch (2 L) square glass baking dish. Cover with half of the meat sauce. Repeat layers. Spoon cottage cheese over top, spreading evenly. Sprinkle with provolone cheese. *Make-ahead: Cover and refrigerate for up to 24 hours.*

← Bake in 375°F (190°C) oven until bubbly and golden, about 30 minutes.

PER EACH OF 6 SERVINGS: about 409 cal, 28 g pro, 17 g total fat (7 g sat. fat) 35 g carb, 4 g fibre, 55 mg chol, 909 mg sodium.

% RDI: 13% calcium, 23% iron, 10% vit A, 45% vit C, 27% folate.

STOVE-TOP TUNA CASSEROLE

102 →

A few cans of tuna in the cupboard are lifesavers on a busy night. The solid white tuna is best for taste and chunkiness, but you can use any kind you have on hand.

Makes 4 servings

12 oz	linguine	**375 g**
4 cups	frozen mixed Asian- or Italian-style vegetables	**1 L**
1	can (385 mL) 2% evaporated milk	**1**
⅔ cup	grated Parmesan cheese	**150 mL**
1 tbsp	lemon juice	**15 mL**
1	large clove garlic, minced	**1**
½ tsp	each dry mustard, dried oregano and salt	**2 mL**
¼ tsp	pepper	**1 mL**
2	cans (each 6 oz/170 g) solid white tuna, drained	**2**

← In large pot of boiling salted water, cook pasta for 7 minutes. Add vegetables; cook until pasta is tender but firm, about 2 minutes. Drain in colander.
← In same pot, whisk together milk, cheese, lemon juice, garlic, mustard, oregano, salt and pepper over medium heat until smooth and hot. Break tuna into chunks; add to pot along with pasta mixture. Stir to coat and heat through.

PER SERVING: about 607 cal, 45 g pro, 10 g total fat (5 g sat. fat), 83 g carb, 5 g fibre, 41 mg chol, 1,187 mg sodium. % RDI: 54% calcium, 32% iron, 22% vit A, 73% vit C, 59% folate.

EGGPLANT AND PEPPER ROTINI

There's enough pasta here to enjoy for dinner one night and reheat the rest for lunch the next day.

Makes 6 servings

1	large eggplant (about 1 lb/500 g)	1
¾ tsp	salt	4 mL
2 tbsp	extra-virgin olive oil	25 mL
1	sweet yellow pepper, chopped	1
½ cup	pine nuts or slivered almonds (optional)	125 mL
8	cloves garlic, minced	8
¼ tsp	hot pepper flakes	1 mL
2	cans (each 19 oz/540 mL) tomatoes	2
⅓ cup	tomato paste	75 mL
7 cups	rotini (1½ lb/750 g)	1.75 L
½ cup	chopped fresh parsley	125 mL
½ cup	grated Parmesan cheese	125 mL

◄105

← Cut eggplant into generous ¼-inch (5 mm) thick slices; place in large bowl. Sprinkle with salt and toss; let stand for 15 minutes. Using towels, wipe off salt and pat slices dry; cut into quarters.

← In large shallow Dutch oven, heat oil over medium heat; fry eggplant, stirring occasionally, until golden and tender, about 8 minutes.

← Add yellow pepper, pine nuts (if using), garlic and hot pepper flakes; fry, stirring, until garlic is fragrant, about 2 minutes.

← Add tomatoes and tomato paste, breaking up with spoon; bring to boil. Reduce heat and simmer until thickened enough to mound on spoon, about 15 minutes.

← Meanwhile, in large pot of boiling salted water, cook pasta until tender but firm, 8 to 10 minutes. Drain and return to pot. Add sauce along with parsley; toss to coat. Sprinkle with Parmesan cheese. *Make-ahead: Let cool for 30 minutes; refrigerate, uncovered, in airtight container until cold. Cover and refrigerate for up to 24 hours.*

PER SERVING: about 583 cal, 21 g pro, 10 g total fat (3 g sat. fat), 104 g carb, 9 g fibre, 7 mg chol, 738 mg sodium. % RDI: 20% calcium, 34% iron, 19% vit A, 113% vit C, 88% folate.

BUCATINI WITH ROASTED GARLIC AND CHERRY TOMATOES

106 →

Roasting tomatoes brings out their rich flavour, and using cherry tomatoes speeds up the process.

Makes 4 to 6 servings

4 cups	cherry tomatoes, halved	**1 L**
12	cloves garlic, halved	**12**
¼ cup	extra-virgin olive oil	**50 mL**
1 tsp	dried basil	**5 mL**
½ tsp	salt	**2 mL**
¼ tsp	each hot pepper flakes and pepper	**1 mL**
1 lb	bucatini	**500 g**
¼ cup	chopped fresh parsley	**50 mL**
½ cup	shaved Parmesan cheese	**125 mL**

 In 13- x 9-inch (3.5 L) metal cake pan, toss together tomatoes, garlic, oil, basil, salt, hot pepper flakes and pepper; roast in 400°F (200°C) oven until tomatoes are shrivelled and garlic is tender, about 30 minutes.

 Meanwhile, in large pot of boiling salted water, cook pasta until tender but firm, 8 to 10 minutes. Drain and return to pot. Add tomato mixture and parsley; toss to coat. Serve sprinkled with Parmesan.

PER EACH OF 6 SERVINGS: about 424 cal, 14 g pro, 13 g total fat (3 g sat. fat), 62 g carb, 4 g fibre, 7 mg chol, 554 mg sodium. % RDI: 14% calcium, 18% iron, 12% vit A, 27% vit C, 52% folate.

TIP

For the Parmesan, a piece of Parmigiano-Reggiano has the best flavour and shaves nicely over the pasta. You can substitute other sharp hard cheeses, such as grana Padano, Romano or Asiago.

STEAK STIR-FRY WITH NOODLES

108 →

You can also use boneless chicken breasts or pork tenderloin instead of beef for this one-wok stir-fry.

Makes 4 servings

1 lb	top sirloin grilling steak, thinly sliced	500 g
¼ tsp	each salt and pepper	1 mL
2 tbsp	vegetable oil	25 mL
1	onion, sliced	1
2	cloves garlic, minced	2
3	carrots, thinly sliced	3
1	sweet green pepper, thinly sliced	1
¾ cup	beef stock	175 mL
1 tsp	grated orange rind	5 mL
¼ cup	orange juice	50 mL
1 tbsp	cornstarch	15 mL
¾ tsp	hot pepper sauce	4 mL
¼ cup	chopped fresh parsley	50 mL
8 oz	linguine	250 g

← Season steak with salt and pepper. In wok or large skillet, heat half of the oil over high heat; stir-fry steak, in batches, until browned but still pink inside, about 2 minutes. Transfer to plate.

← Heat remaining oil in wok over medium heat; stir-fry onion and garlic for 2 minutes. Add carrots and green pepper; stir-fry until slightly softened, about 4 minutes.

← Whisk together beef stock, orange rind and juice, cornstarch and hot pepper sauce; add to wok and bring to boil. Return meat and any accumulated juices to wok along with parsley.

← Meanwhile, in large pot of boiling salted water, cook linguine until tender but firm, 6 to 8 minutes; drain and add to wok. Toss to coat well.

PER SERVING: about 478 cal, 33 g pro, 12 g total fat (2 g sat. fat), 57 g carb, 5 g fibre, 54 mg chol, 555 mg sodium. % RDI: 6% calcium, 34% iron, 140% vit A, 55% vit C, 50% folate.

WORLD-FAMOUS MACARONI AND CHEESE

This dish is the most popular one on the menu of Mike's Quick Lunch in Sault Ste. Marie, Ont. The sauce makes enough for leftovers you can use for meatball or sausage sandwiches or your favourite pasta dish.

Makes 6 to 8 servings

2 tbsp	vegetable oil	25 mL
2	stalks celery, diced	2
1	onion, chopped	1
Half	sweet green pepper, diced	Half
2 tsp	dried basil	10 mL
½ cup	tomato paste	125 mL
2	cans (each 28 oz/796 mL) tomatoes, chopped	2
1	can (28 oz/796 mL) crushed tomatoes	1
½ tsp	each salt and pepper	2 mL
6 cups	medium pasta shells (about 1 lb/500 g)	1.5 L
9	slices processed Cheddar cheese	9
9	slices processed mozzarella or Swiss cheese	9

In large Dutch oven, heat oil over medium heat; fry celery, onion, green pepper and basil, stirring occasionally, until softened, about 8 minutes.

← Add tomato paste; cook for 5 minutes, stirring occasionally. Add chopped and crushed tomatoes, salt and pepper; bring to boil. Reduce heat, cover and simmer for 2 hours.

← Uncover and simmer until sauce holds ripple when pushed, about 1 hour. *Make-ahead: Let cool for 30 minutes. Refrigerate, uncovered, in airtight container until cold; cover and refrigerate for up to 3 days or freeze for up to 2 weeks.*

← In large pot of boiling salted water, cook pasta until tender but firm, about 8 minutes. Drain and return to pot. Add 2 cups (500 mL) of the tomato sauce; toss to coat.

← Ladle 1½ cups (375 mL) more sauce into 13- x 9-inch (3 L) glass baking dish; spread half of the pasta over top. Repeat layers once; top with 1 cup (250 mL) more sauce. *Make-ahead: Cover and refrigerate for up to 24 hours; uncover and bake in 350°F (180°C) oven until hot, about 40 minutes.* Reserve remaining sauce for another use.

← Overlapping slightly, arrange Cheddar and mozzarella cheeses evenly over top; bake in 425°F (220°C) oven until cheese melts, about 5 minutes.

PER EACH OF 8 SERVINGS: about 573 cal, 25 g pro, 21 g total fat (8 g sat. fat), 73 g carb, 8 g fibre, 41 mg chol, 1,246 mg sodium.
% RDI: 45% calcium, 34% iron, 35% vit A, 70% vit C, 57% folate.

WORLD-FAMOUS MACARONI AND CHEESE

This dish is the most popular one on the menu of Mike's Quick Lunch in Sault Ste. Marie, Ont. The sauce makes enough for leftovers you can use for meatball or sausage sandwiches or your favourite pasta dish.

Makes 6 to 8 servings

2 tbsp	vegetable oil	**25 mL**
2	stalks celery, diced	**2**
1	onion, chopped	**1**
Half	sweet green pepper, diced	**Half**
2 tsp	dried basil	**10 mL**
½ cup	tomato paste	**125 mL**
2	cans (each 28 oz/796 mL) tomatoes, chopped	**2**
1	can (28 oz/796 mL) crushed tomatoes	**1**
½ tsp	each salt and pepper	**2 mL**
6 cups	medium pasta shells (about 1 lb/500 g)	**1.5 L**
9	slices processed Cheddar cheese	**9**
9	slices processed mozzarella or Swiss cheese	**9**

← In large Dutch oven, heat oil over medium heat; fry celery, onion, green pepper and basil, stirring occasionally, until softened, about 8 minutes.

← Add tomato paste; cook for 5 minutes, stirring occasionally. Add chopped and crushed tomatoes, salt and pepper; bring to boil. Reduce heat, cover and simmer for 2 hours.

← Uncover and simmer until sauce holds ripple when pushed, about 1 hour. *Make-ahead: Let cool for 30 minutes Refrigerate, uncovered, in airtight container until cold; cover and refrigerate for up to 3 days or freeze for up to 2 weeks.*

← In large pot of boiling salted water, cook pasta until tender but firm, about 8 minutes. Drain and return to pot. Add 2 cups (500 mL) of the tomato sauce; toss to coat.

← Ladle 1½ cups (375 mL) more sauce into 13- x 9-inch (3 L) glass baking dish; spread half of the pasta over top. Repeat layers once; top with 1 cup (250 mL) more sauce. *Make-ahead: Cover and refrigerate for up to 24 hours; uncover and bake in 350°F (180°C) oven until hot, about 40 minutes.* Reserve remaining sauce for another use.

← Overlapping slightly, arrange Cheddar and mozzarella cheeses evenly over top; bake in 425°F (220°C) oven until cheese melts, about 5 minutes.

PER EACH OF 8 SERVINGS: about 573 cal, 25 g pro, 21 g total fat (8 g sat. fat), 73 g carb, 8 g fibre, 41 mg chol, 1,246 mg sodium.

% RDI: 45% calcium, 34% iron, 35% vit A, 70% vit C, 57% folate.

KIDS' FAVOURITE SALMON PASTA WITH PEAS

This dish takes only minutes to make. While frozen peas are a vegetable kids really like, there are other choices, such as frozen cut broccoli, green beans or frozen mixed vegetables.

Makes 4 servings

5 cups	farfalle (1 lb/500 g)	**1.25 L**
1 tsp	vegetable oil	**5 mL**
2	green onions, chopped	**2**
2	cloves garlic, minced	**2**
1⅔ cups	milk	**400 mL**
2 tbsp	cornstarch	**25 mL**
1 cup	frozen peas	**250 mL**
½ cup	light cream cheese, cubed	**125 mL**
2 tbsp	chopped fresh parsley	**25 mL**
2 tbsp	lemon juice	**25 mL**
1 tbsp	Dijon mustard	**15 mL**
1 tsp	dried dillweed	**5 mL**
¼ tsp	each salt and pepper	**1 mL**
1	can (7.5 oz/213 g) sockeye salmon, drained and broken into chunks	**1**

← 113

← In large pot of boiling salted water, cook pasta until tender but firm, 8 to 10 minutes. Reserving ½ cup (125 mL) of the cooking liquid, drain and return pasta to pot.

← Meanwhile, in saucepan, heat oil over medium heat; fry onions and garlic, stirring occasionally, until softened, about 2 minutes. Add milk; heat until steaming. Whisk cornstarch with 2 tbsp (25 mL) water; stir into milk mixture and cook, stirring, until thickened, 2 to 3 minutes.

← Add peas, cheese, parsley, lemon juice, mustard, dillweed, salt and pepper; stir until cheese is melted. Add to pasta and toss to coat, adding reserved cooking liquid if desired. Add salmon; toss gently.

PER SERVING: about 646 cal, 29 g pro, 13 g total fat (6 g sat. fat), 100 g carb, 7 g fibre, 37 mg chol, 790 mg sodium. % RDI: 27% calcium, 29% iron, 16% vit A, 15% vit C, 88% folate.

ORECCHIETTE WITH BROCCOLI AND GARLIC

Frying garlic just until it is slightly golden gives it a nutty, slightly spicy flavour that marries well with broccoli. But watch the garlic carefully because if it goes beyond golden, it becomes bitter.

Makes 4 to 6 servings

1	bunch broccoli	1
4 cups	orecchiette or small shell pasta (12 oz/375 g)	1 L
2 tbsp	extra-virgin olive oil	25 mL
8	cloves garlic, thinly sliced	8
6	anchovy fillets, chopped (or 1 tbsp/15 mL anchovy paste)	6
½ tsp	hot pepper flakes	2 mL
¼ tsp	salt	1 mL
¼ cup	grated Parmesan cheese	50 mL

← Cut broccoli into small florets; peel and chop stems. In large pot of boiling salted water, cover and cook broccoli until tender-crisp, about 2 minutes. With slotted spoon, transfer to bowl of ice water. Drain and set aside.

← In same pot of boiling salted water, cook pasta until tender but firm, 8 to 10 minutes. Reserving ½ cup (125 mL) of the cooking liquid, drain and return to pot.

← Meanwhile, in skillet, heat oil over medium heat; fry garlic, anchovies, hot pepper flakes and salt, stirring occasionally, until garlic is fragrant and anchovies begin to break down, about 2 minutes.

← Add broccoli to skillet; cook until heated through and garlic starts to turn golden, about 2 minutes. Add to pasta along with reserved cooking liquid; toss to coat. Serve sprinkled with Parmesan cheese.

PER EACH OF 6 SERVINGS: about 305 cal, 13 g pro, 7 g total fat (2 g sat. fat), 48 g carb, 4 g fibre, 7 mg chol, 699 mg sodium. % RDI: 11% calcium, 15% iron, 12% vit A, 97% vit C, 54% folate.

TIP

Pasta does not wait, so warm the serving bowls while the pasta boils.

LEMON PARMESAN LINGUINE

116 →

This dish can become the foundation for year-round dinners. Add fresh herbs during summer and dried thyme or oregano when it's cold. Try Parmigiano-Reggiano, grana Padano or Pecorino Romano. For the photo we used shelled edamame (green soybeans, available frozen) instead of green beans.

Makes 4 servings

12 oz	whole wheat or regular linguine	**375 g**
3 cups	chopped green beans	**750 mL**
¼ cup	slivered almonds	**50 mL**
2 tbsp	extra-virgin olive oil	**25 mL**
Half	red onion, thinly sliced	**Half**
2	cloves garlic, minced	**2**
2 tsp	chopped fresh thyme	**10 mL**
1 tsp	grated lemon rind	**5 mL**
½ tsp	each salt and pepper	**2 mL**
⅓ cup	grated Parmesan cheese	**75 mL**
¼ cup	lemon juice	**50 mL**

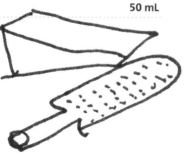

← In large pot of boiling salted water, cook pasta for 6 minutes. Add green beans; cook until pasta is tender but firm, about 4 minutes. Drain and return to pot, reserving ½ cup (125 mL) of the cooking liquid.

← Meanwhile, in large skillet, toast almonds over medium heat until golden, about 3 minutes; remove and set aside.

← Add oil to skillet; fry onion, garlic, thyme, lemon rind, salt and pepper over medium heat, stirring occasionally, until onion is softened, about 2 minutes. Add to pasta along with Parmesan cheese, lemon juice and reserved cooking liquid; toss to coat. Serve sprinkled with almonds.

PER SERVING: about 489 cal, 20 g pro, 15 g total fat (3 g sat. fat), 77 g carb, 11 g fibre, 7 mg chol, 928 mg sodium. % RDI: 20% calcium, 30% iron, 7% vit A, 30% vit C, 22% folate.

GOLDEN STIR-FRY NOODLES

Tofu, made from soybeans, adds a good source of protein to a meatless meal. The recipe calls for precooked Chinese noodles, now supermarket available, but you can use 8 oz (250 g) linguine, cooked, as a perfectly fine substitute.

Makes 4 servings

1 tsp	vegetable oil	5 mL
1	onion, sliced	1
1 tbsp	mild curry paste	15 mL
1 cup	vegetable stock	250 mL
½ cup	mango chutney	125 mL
1	bag (500 g) frozen mixed chopped broccoli, carrots and cauliflower	1
1	pkg (400 g) precooked Chinese noodles	1
1 cup	chopped extra-firm tofu or cooked chicken	250 mL
¼ cup	unsalted peanuts	50 mL
2 tbsp	chopped fresh coriander, basil or mint (optional)	25 mL

← In wok or large saucepan, heat oil over medium-high heat; fry onion, stirring often, until softened, about 5 minutes. ←119

← Stir in curry paste; cook for 30 seconds. Stir in stock and chutney; bring to boil. Add vegetables; cook for 3 minutes.

← Under warm running water, loosen noodles; add to wok. Add tofu; cook over medium heat, stirring, for 5 minutes. Serve sprinkled with peanuts, and coriander (if using).

PER SERVING: about 519 cal, 22 g pro, 11 g total fat (1 g sat. fat), 87 g carb, 8 g fibre, 73 mg chol, 283 mg sodium. % RDI: 14% calcium, 27% iron, 90% vit A, 33% vit C, 38% folate.

TIP

Instead of tofu, you can use cooked chicken.

LASAGNA TOSS

Instead of taking the time to layer lasagna, capture the dish's classic flavours by tossing everything together in a pot. Parmesan and Romano cheeses are excellent substitutes if you can't find Asiago.

Makes 4 servings

12 oz	lean ground beef	375 g
1	onion, chopped	1
2	cloves garlic, minced	2
6 cups	quartered mushrooms (about 1 lb/500 g)	1.5 L
2 tsp	dried Italian herb seasoning	10 mL
¼ tsp	each salt and pepper	1 mL
1	jar (750 mL) pasta sauce	1
1	sweet green pepper, chopped	1
12 oz	lasagna noodles	375 g
1 tbsp	balsamic or wine vinegar	15 mL
⅓ cup	shredded Asiago cheese	75 mL

←121

In nonstick skillet, sauté beef over medium-high heat, breaking up with spoon, until no longer pink, about 7 minutes. With slotted spoon, transfer meat to bowl. Drain any fat from pan.

Add onion, garlic, mushrooms, herb seasoning, salt and pepper to pan; fry over medium heat, stirring occasionally, until mushrooms are browned and liquid is evaporated, 10 minutes.

Return meat to pan. Add pasta sauce and green pepper; simmer until pepper is tender, 10 minutes.

Meanwhile, break each noodle into quarters. In large pot of boiling salted water, cook pasta until tender but firm, about 8 minutes. Reserving ½ cup (125 mL) of the cooking liquid, drain and return to pot. Add sauce and vinegar. Add reserved pasta water to further moisten if desired; toss to coat. Serve sprinkled with cheese.

PER SERVING: about 716 cal, 34 g pro, 18 g total fat (6 g sat. fat), 106 g carb, 10 g fibre, 50 mg chol, 1,473 mg sodium. % RDI: 15% calcium, 46% iron, 27% vit A, 73% vit C, 80% folate.

TIP

You can add a dollop of light ricotta cheese to each serving.

20-MINUTE SAUSAGE CACCIATORE

122 →

Everybody loves pasta, particularly when it's tossed with a sauce that's chunky with sausage and vegetables.

Makes 4 servings

1 tbsp	vegetable oil	**15 mL**
1	onion, thinly sliced	**1**
1	sweet green pepper, sliced	**1**
2 cups	quartered mushrooms	**500 mL**
2	carrots, sliced	**2**
4	cloves garlic, minced	**4**
½ tsp	dried oregano	**2 mL**
¼ tsp	each salt and pepper	**1 mL**
1	can (19 oz/540 mL) tomatoes	**1**
¼ cup	tomato paste	**50 mL**
3	lean Italian sausages (12 oz/375 g)	**3**
4 cups	rotini (about 12 oz/375 g)	**1 L**
¼ cup	grated Romano cheese	**50 mL**

← In saucepan, heat oil over medium heat; fry onion, green pepper, mushrooms, carrots, garlic, oregano, salt and pepper until liquid from mushrooms is evaporated, about 8 minutes.

← Add tomatoes and tomato paste; bring to boil, stirring. Reduce heat and simmer for 10 minutes.

← Meanwhile, prick sausages all over with fork. In skillet, cook sausages over medium-high heat, turning occasionally, until browned outside and no longer pink inside, about 10 minutes. Drain on paper towels; slice thinly. Add to tomato mixture; simmer until thickened and bubbly, about 10 minutes.

← Meanwhile, in large pot of boiling salted water, cook pasta until tender but firm, 8 to 10 minutes; drain and return to pot. Add sauce and toss to coat. Serve sprinkled with Romano cheese.

PER SERVING: about 501 cal, 25 g pro, 19 g total fat (6 g sat. fat), 58 g carb, 7 g fibre, 46 mg chol, 1,228 mg sodium. % RDI: 18% calcium, 31% iron, 106% vit A, 85% vit C, 45% folate.

SPAGHETTI WITH PUTTANESCA SAUCE

Anchovies, olives and capers make this quick tomato sauce robust. As a bonus, you can freeze the sauce to have on hand for busy-night meals.

Makes 4 servings

1 tbsp	extra-virgin olive oil	15 mL
4	cloves garlic, minced	4
½ tsp	dried oregano	2 mL
¼ tsp	hot pepper flakes	1 mL
4	anchovy fillets, chopped (or 2 tsp/10 mL anchovy paste)	4
1	can (28 oz/796 mL) tomatoes	1
½ cup	oil-cured olives, halved and pitted	125 mL
2 tbsp	drained rinsed capers	25 mL
¼ cup	chopped fresh parsley	50 mL
1 lb	spaghetti or other long pasta	500 g

←125

← In large skillet, heat oil over medium heat; fry garlic, oregano, hot pepper flakes and anchovies, stirring occasionally, until garlic starts to colour, about 3 minutes.

← Add tomatoes, breaking up with spoon. Add olives and capers; bring to boil. Reduce heat and simmer until thickened to consistency of salsa, about 10 minutes. *Make-ahead: Let cool for 20 minutes. Refrigerate, uncovered, in airtight container until cold; cover and refrigerate for up to 2 days or freeze for up to 1 month.* Stir in parsley.

← Meanwhile, in large pot of boiling salted water, cook pasta until tender but firm, 8 to 10 minutes; drain and return to pot. Add sauce and toss to coat.

PER SERVING: about 561 cal, 18 g pro, 12 g total fat (2 g sat. fat), 96 g carb, 8 g fibre, 3 mg chol, 1,430 mg sodium. % RDI: 11% calcium, 31% iron, 14% vit A, 53% vit C, 80% folate.

PAD THAI

This noodle dish is popular on both take-out and restaurant menus. Even though it requires a fair amount of chopping, the meal is worth every minute. Kids who turn up their noses at pasta with sauce can't get enough of Pad Thai.

Makes 6 servings

6 oz	rice stick noodles	175 g
⅓ cup	chili sauce	75 mL
¼ cup	fish sauce	50 mL
¼ cup	lime juice	50 mL
1 tsp	Asian chili paste or hot pepper sauce	5 mL
2 tbsp	vegetable oil	25 mL
6	cloves garlic, minced	6
4	shallots (or 1 onion), sliced	4
1	each sweet green and red pepper, sliced	1
12 oz	large shrimp, peeled and deveined	375 g
1	egg, lightly beaten	1
4 oz	medium tofu, cubed	125 g
2 cups	bean sprouts	500 mL
6	green onions, sliced	6
½ cup	chopped fresh coriander	125 mL
½ cup	chopped roasted peanuts	125 mL
	Coriander sprigs and lime wedges	

← In large bowl, soak noodles in warm water until flexible, about 15 minutes; drain and place in large dry bowl. Set aside.

← Meanwhile, in small bowl, mix together ½ cup (125 mL) water, chili sauce, fish sauce, lime juice and chili paste; set aside.

← In wok, heat 1 tbsp (15 mL) of the oil over medium-high heat; stir-fry garlic, shallots and green and red peppers until softened, about 4 minutes. Add to noodles.

← Add remaining oil to wok; stir-fry shrimp until pink, about 2 minutes. Add fish sauce mixture and bring to boil; reduce heat to medium. Stir in egg; cook, stirring, until sauce is thickened, about 1 minute.

← Add noodle mixture, tofu, bean sprouts, green onions and chopped coriander; toss and stir-fry until noodles are tender, about 3 minutes. Garnish with peanuts, coriander sprigs and lime wedges.

PER SERVING: about 331 cal, 20 g pro, 11 g total fat (2 g sat. fat), 39 g carb, 4 g fibre, 117 mg chol, 915 mg sodium. % RDI: 9% calcium, 21% iron, 15% vit A, 97% vit C, 31% folate.

NOODLES AND CHICKEN WITH PEANUT SAUCE

It only takes a few minutes to toss this dish together.

Makes 4 servings

12 oz	whole wheat spaghetti	375 g
2	carrots, halved and thinly sliced	2
2 tsp	vegetable oil	10 mL
2	boneless skinless chicken breasts, sliced	2
⅓ cup	hoisin sauce	75 mL
¼ cup	smooth peanut butter	50 mL
2 tbsp	cider vinegar	25 mL
1	clove garlic, minced	1
½ tsp	hot pepper sauce	2 mL
4 cups	shredded leaf lettuce (optional)	1 L
1½ cups	bean sprouts	375 mL
1 cup	chopped fresh coriander or parsley	250 mL
⅔ cup	thinly sliced red onion	150 mL
¼ cup	chopped roasted peanuts	50 mL

← In large pot of boiling salted water, cook spaghetti until tender but firm, about 8 minutes. Add carrots; cook for 30 seconds. Drain and rinse under cold water; set aside in colander.

← Meanwhile, in large skillet, heat oil over medium-high heat; stir-fry chicken until browned and no longer pink inside, 4 minutes.

← In large bowl, whisk together ½ cup (125 mL) water, hoisin sauce, peanut butter, vinegar, garlic and hot pepper sauce until smooth. Add pasta mixture, chicken and any accumulated juices, lettuce (if using), bean sprouts, ¾ cup (175 mL) of the coriander and onion; toss to combine. Sprinkle with peanuts and remaining coriander.

PER SERVING: about 624 cal, 37 g pro, 18 g total fat (3 g sat. fat), 86 g carb, 12 g fibre, 39 mg chol, 861 mg sodium. % RDI: 8% calcium, 31% iron, 93% vit A, 15% vit C, 34% folate.

CREAMY WALNUT PASTA SHELLS

Blue cheese accents the creaminess of the sauce, and walnuts give the dish body. Choose California walnuts for their freshness.

Makes 4 servings

⅓ cup	chopped walnut halves	**75 mL**
2 tbsp	butter	**25 mL**
2 tsp	chopped fresh thyme (or ½ tsp/2 mL dried)	**10 mL**
¾ cup	10% cream	**175 mL**
4 oz	blue cheese, Stilton or Gorgonzola cheese, crumbled or cubed	**125 g**
Pinch	pepper	**Pinch**
4 cups	medium-size shell pasta (about 12 oz/375 g)	**1 L**
2 tbsp	chopped fresh parsley	**25 mL**

← In large skillet, toast walnuts over medium heat, stirring occasionally, until fragrant, 5 to 7 minutes.
← Add butter and thyme; cook for 30 seconds. Add cream, blue cheese and pepper; simmer over medium-low heat, stirring occasionally, until slightly thickened and cheese melts, about 5 minutes.
← Meanwhile, in large pot of boiling salted water, cook pasta until tender but firm, 8 to 10 minutes; drain well and return to pot. Add sauce; toss to coat. Serve sprinkled with parsley.

PER SERVING: about 587 cal, 20 g pro, 26 g total fat (12 g sat. fat), 68 g carb, 4 g fibre, 51 mg chol, 698 mg sodium. % RDI: 21% calcium, 18% iron, 17% vit A, 3% vit C, 63% folate.

LEMONY CHICKEN PASTA

You don't need a lot of chicken to rustle up this light-tasting but satisfying dish. Get someone to make a salad to serve before the main dish.

Makes 4 servings

4 cups	penne (12 oz/375 g)	1 L
12 oz	boneless skinless chicken breasts	375 g
1 tbsp	butter	15 mL
3	cloves garlic, minced	3
1 cup	light ricotta cheese	250 mL
¼ cup	grated Parmesan cheese	50 mL
1 tsp	grated lemon rind	5 mL
2 tbsp	lemon juice	25 mL
½ tsp	salt	2 mL
¼ tsp	pepper	1 mL
Pinch	nutmeg	Pinch
4 cups	packed trimmed spinach, shredded	1 L

←133

← In large pot of boiling salted water, cook pasta until tender but firm, 8 to 10 minutes. Drain and return to pot, reserving ½ cup (125 mL) of the cooking liquid.

← Meanwhile, cut chicken crosswise into slices. In nonstick skillet, melt butter over medium-high heat; brown chicken, stirring occasionally, about 5 minutes. Add garlic; cook, stirring, for 1 minute.

← Add reserved cooking liquid, ricotta cheese, half of the Parmesan cheese, the lemon rind and juice, salt, pepper and nutmeg; bring to simmer.

← Add spinach; stir until wilted. Add to pasta and toss to coat. Serve sprinkled with remaining Parmesan cheese.

PER SERVING: about 568 cal, 41 g pro, 13 g total fat (7 g sat. fat), 70 g carb, 5 g fibre, 81 mg chol, 819 mg sodium. % RDI: 32% calcium, 32% iron, 54% vit A, 17% vit C, 94% folate.

CHAPTER 5
VEGETA

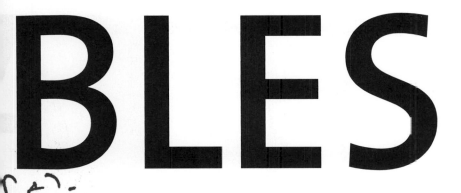

BLES

← 137

STEAMED ASPARAGUS WITH ORANGE VINAIGRETTE

140 →

Tender-crisp asparagus dresses up any menu. Choose straight, tall firm green stalks with tightly closed, purple-tinged tips. You could also use this vinaigrette as a dipping sauce for chilled asparagus.

Makes 4 servings

2 lb	asparagus	1 kg
ORANGE VINAIGRETTE		
¼ cup	light mayonnaise	50 mL
1 tsp	grated orange rind	5 mL
1 tbsp	orange juice	15 mL
Pinch	each salt and pepper	Pinch

← Snap off tough woody ends of asparagus. Place in steamer over boiling water; cover and steam until tender-crisp, about 4 minutes. Arrange on serving plate.

← **ORANGE VINAIGRETTE:** Meanwhile, in small bowl, whisk together mayonnaise, orange rind and juice, salt and pepper; drizzle over asparagus.

PER SERVING: about 86 cal, 4 g pro, 5 g total fat (1 g sat. fat), 8 g carb, 3 g fibre, 5 mg chol, 127 mg sodium. % RDI: 3% calcium, 9% iron, 9% vit A, 33% vit C, 105% folate.

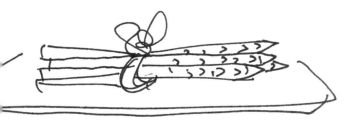

TIP

Use any of the these methods to cook asparagus just until tender-crisp. Then enjoy the stalks simply seasoned with salt, pepper and a little olive oil or butter, or just a drizzle of vinaigrette (as on this page) or a favourite salad dressing.

← **TO BOIL:** Bring pot of salted water to boil before adding asparagus; cover and boil for about 3 minutes. Or stand asparagus in 1 inch (2.5 cm) boiling water in tall saucepan; cover and boil for about 3 minutes.

← **TO GRILL:** In shallow dish, brush or roll asparagus with 1 tbsp (15 mL) vegetable oil. Place on greased grill over medium-high heat; close lid and grill for about 7 minutes, turning once.

← **TO ROAST:** Arrange asparagus on rimmed baking sheet; drizzle with 1 tbsp (15 mL) vegetable oil and roll to coat. Roast in 500°F (260°C) oven for about 5 minutes, shaking pan once.

CRUNCHY BROCCOLI AND FETA SALAD

Lightly steaming broccoli turns this supernutritious vegetable bright green. This salad is perfect for a buffet, picnic, packed lunch or potluck party.

Makes 4 to 6 servings

1	bunch broccoli (about 1 lb/500 g)	1
2 tbsp	extra-virgin olive oil	25 mL
2 tbsp	wine vinegar	25 mL
2 tsp	Dijon mustard	10 mL
1	clove garlic, minced	1
¼ tsp	each salt and pepper	1 mL
1 cup	crumbled feta cheese	250 mL
1 cup	grape or cherry tomatoes, halved	250 mL
½ cup	thinly sliced red onion	125 mL

← Cut broccoli into florets; peel and cut stems into ¼-inch (5 mm) thick slices. Place in steamer over boiling water; cover and steam until bright green but still crisp, about 1 minute. Drain.

← In large bowl, whisk together oil, vinegar, mustard, garlic, salt and pepper. Add broccoli, feta cheese, tomatoes and onion; toss to coat.
Make-ahead: Cover and refrigerate for up to 24 hours.

PER EACH OF 6 SERVINGS: about 127 cal, 6 g pro, 9 g total fat (4 g sat. fat), 7 g carb, 2 g fibre, 18 mg chol, 371 mg sodium.

% RDI: 13% calcium, 7% iron, 14% vit A, 102% vit C, 22% folate.

TWO TOSSES
FOR BROCCOLI

These quick and easy hot side dishes show off broccoli delectably.

←143

GARLIC BROCCOLI TOSS

Makes 4 servings

1	bunch broccoli (about 1 lb/500 g)	1
1 tbsp	vegetable oil	15 mL
2	cloves garlic, minced	2
¼ tsp	each salt and pepper	1 mL

← Cut broccoli into florets; peel and cut stems into ¼-inch (5 mm) thick slices. Place in steamer or in saucepan of boiling salted water; cover and cook until bright green but still crisp, about 3 minutes. Drain well.

← Meanwhile, in skillet, heat oil over medium heat; fry garlic, salt and pepper until fragrant. Add broccoli; toss to coat.

PER SERVING: about 64 cal, 4 g pro, 4 g total fat (trace sat. fat), 6 g carb, 3 g fibre, 0 mg chol, 441 mg sodium. % RDI: 5% calcium, 7% iron, 16% vit A, 142% vit C, 26% folate.

ASIAN BROCCOLI TOSS

Makes 4 servings

1	bunch broccoli (about 1 lb/500 g)	1
1 tbsp	vegetable oil	15 mL
1 tsp	minced gingerroot	5 mL
1	clove garlic, minced	1
¼ tsp	pepper	1 mL
1 tbsp	oyster sauce	15 mL

← Cut broccoli into florets; peel and cut stems into ¼-inch (5 mm) thick slices. Place in steamer or in saucepan of boiling salted water; cover and cook until bright green but still crisp, about 3 minutes. Drain well.

← Meanwhile, in skillet, heat oil over medium heat; fry ginger, garlic and pepper until fragrant. Add broccoli and oyster sauce; toss to coat.

PER SERVING: about 66 cal, 4 g pro, 4 g total fat (trace sat. fat), 7 g carb, 3 g fibre, 0 mg chol, 419 mg sodium. % RDI: 5% calcium, 7% iron, 16% vit A, 142% vit C, 25% folate.

GOLDEN CAULIFLOWER AND CHEESE CASSEROLE

144 → This crusty sauce-covered cauliflower dish is excellent with Cheddar cheese, but Gruyère is just as good.

Makes 4 servings

1	large cauliflower (about 2¾ lb/1.375 kg)	1
2 tbsp	butter	25 mL
1	small onion, minced	1
⅓ cup	all-purpose flour	75 mL
4 cups	hot milk	1 L
1½ cups	shredded old Cheddar cheese	375 mL
½ tsp	dry mustard	2 mL
½ tsp	each salt and pepper	2 mL
¼ cup	fresh or dry bread crumbs	50 mL
¼ cup	grated Parmesan cheese	50 mL
2 tbsp	chopped fresh parsley	25 mL

← Cut cauliflower into bite-size florets. Place in steamer over boiling water; cover and steam until tender, about 10 minutes. Transfer to 8-inch (2 L) square glass baking dish.

← Meanwhile, in saucepan, melt butter over medium heat; fry onion, stirring occasionally, until softened, about 5 minutes. Stir in flour; cook, stirring, until light golden, 1 minute. Whisk in milk, ½ cup (125 mL) at a time; simmer, whisking, until thick enough to coat back of spoon, about 8 minutes. Stir in Cheddar cheese, mustard, salt and pepper; until cheese is melted. Pour over cauliflower.

← In small bowl, mix together bread crumbs, Parmesan cheese and parsley; sprinkle over cauliflower mixture. Bake in 400°F (200°C) oven until bubbly and light golden, about 15 minutes.

PER SERVING: about 464 cal, 26 g pro, 27 g total fat (17 g sat. fat), 30 g carb, 5 g fibre, 86 mg chol, 888 mg sodium. % RDI: 66% calcium, 13% iron, 31% vit A, 130% vit C, 50% folate.

MINT RED PEPPER PEAS

Frozen peas are a go-with-anything vegetable that requires no preparation — the answer to many a rush-hour challenge.

Makes 4 servings

2 cups	frozen peas	**500 mL**
Half	sweet red pepper, diced	**Half**
1 tbsp	butter	**15 mL**
¼ tsp	salt	**1 mL**
¼ tsp	dried mint	**1 mL**
Pinch	pepper	**Pinch**

← In microwaveable dish, cover and cook peas at high until hot, about 3 minutes. Stir in red pepper, butter, salt, mint and pepper.

PER SERVING: about 79 cal, 3 g pro, 3 g total fat (2 g sat. fat), 10 g carb, 3 g fibre, 9 mg chol, 228 mg sodium. % RDI: 2% calcium, 8% iron, 16% vit A, 58% vit C, 19% folate.

VARIATIONS

HONEY ALMOND PEAS

Substitute ⅓ cup (75 mL) toasted sliced almonds and 1 tsp (5 mL) liquid honey for the red pepper and mint.

GINGER PEPPER PEAS

Substitute 1 tsp (5 mL) sesame oil and ¼ tsp (1 mL) each ground ginger and hot pepper sauce for the red pepper and mint.

LEMON DILL PEAS

Substitute 1 tsp (5 mL) gated lemon rind and ¼ tsp (1 mL) dried dillweed for the red pepper and mint.

SKILLET-STEAMED BRUSSELS SPROUTS

146 →

Just a toss in the pan and a dash of seasoning is all you need for flavourful brussels sprouts.

Makes 4 servings

1 tbsp	butter	**15 mL**
1	clove garlic, minced	**1**
4 cups	brussels sprouts (1 lb/500 g), trimmed and halved	**1 L**
1 tbsp	soy sauce	**15 mL**

← In large skillet, melt butter over medium heat; fry garlic until fragrant, about 30 seconds.

← Add brussels sprouts, 2 tbsp (25 mL) water and soy sauce; cover and cook, stirring occasionally, until tender-crisp, about 10 minutes.

PER SERVING: about 72 cal, 3 g pro, 3 g total fat (2 g sat. fat), 10 g carb, 4 g fibre, 9 mg chol, 311 mg sodium. % RDI: 4% calcium, 10% iron, 11% vit A, 115% vit C, 31% folate.

BRUSSELS SPROUTS WITH MUSTARD SEEDS

The mustard seeds — mild black or brown if you have them — deliver crunch and a bit of a bite to brussels sprouts. Leave them out and you still have a pleasing side dish.

Makes 6 servings

8 cups	small brussels sprouts (about 2 lb/1 kg)	**2 L**
1 tbsp	mustard seeds	**15 mL**
1 tbsp	extra-virgin olive oil	**15 mL**
1	onion, finely chopped	**1**
2	cloves garlic, minced	**2**
¼ tsp	each salt and pepper	**1 mL**
⅓ cup	chicken stock	**75 mL**
1 tbsp	Dijon mustard	**15 mL**
1 tsp	lemon juice	**5 mL**

← Trim outer leaves of brussels sprouts; cut X in bottom of each. In large pot of boiling salted water, cover and cook brussels sprouts until tender-crisp, about 6 minutes. Drain and chill under cold water; drain well. *Make-ahead: Cover and refrigerate for up to 24 hours; add 2 minutes to reheating.*

← In large skillet, toast mustard seeds over medium heat, stirring, until aromatic and seeds begin to pop, about 3 minutes.

← Add oil, onion, garlic, salt and pepper; cook over medium-high heat until softened, about 2 minutes.

← Add brussels sprouts, stock, mustard and lemon juice; cook, tossing occasionally, until heated through and coated, about 2 minutes.

PER SERVING: about 100 cal, 5 g pro, 4 g total fat (1 g sat. fat), 16 g carb, 6 g fibre, 0 mg chol, 594 mg sodium. % RDI: 7% calcium, 15% iron, 11% vit A, 155% vit C, 42% folate.

MAPLE-ROASTED ROOTS

Root vegetables, roasted in a maple-syrup glaze, are welcome at any meal. To ease cleanup, line the baking sheet with greased foil or parchment paper.

← 149

Makes 8 to 10 servings

4	red-skinned potatoes (about 1¼ lb/625 g), unpeeled	4
3	large parsnips, peeled	3
3	large carrots, peeled	3
1	red onion	1
1½ cups	cubed peeled butternut squash	375 mL
2 tbsp	butter, melted	25 mL
¾ tsp	each dried thyme, salt and pepper	4 mL
2 tbsp	maple syrup	25 mL

← Cut potatoes, parsnips and carrots into 1½-inch (4 cm) chunks. Keeping root end of onion intact, trim off roots; cut into 8 wedges.

← In large bowl, toss together potatoes, parsnips, carrots, onion, squash, butter, thyme, salt and pepper; spread on greased large rimmed baking sheet.

← Roast in 450°F (230°C) oven, stirring 3 times, until tender and browned, about 50 minutes. Drizzle with maple syrup, stirring to coat; roast until glazed, about 10 minutes.

PER EACH OF 10 SERVINGS: about 139 cal, 2 g pro, 3 g total fat (1 g sat. fat), 28 g carb, 4 g fibre, 6 mg chol, 220 mg sodium.

% RDI: 4% calcium, 9% iron, 73% vit A, 27% vit C, 19% folate.

PARSNIP PURÉE

Parsnips have a nutty, slightly creamy flavour. Smoky bacon adds a rustic touch, but can, of course, be optional.

←151

Makes 4 to 6 servings

2	bags (each 1 lb/500 g) parsnips	2
1	onion, quartered	1
⅓ cup	light sour cream or plain yogurt	75 mL
½ tsp	each salt and pepper	2 mL
2 tbsp	minced fresh parsley	25 mL
4	strips bacon, cooked and crumbled	4

← Peel parsnips; cut into 1-inch (2.5 cm) cubes. In large pot of boiling salted water, cover and cook parsnips and onion until tender, about 10 minutes. Drain, reserving ¼ cup (50 mL) of the cooking water.
← In food processor, purée together parsnips, onion, reserved cooking water, sour cream, salt and pepper until smooth. Transfer to warmed serving bowl. Stir in half each of the parsley and bacon. Sprinkle with remaining parsley and bacon.

PER EACH OF 6 SERVINGS: about 142 cal, 4 g prc, 3 g total fat (1 g sat. fat), 26 g carb, 4 g fibre, 6 mg chol, 574 mg sodium. % RCI: 7% calcium, 6% iron, 1% vit A, 30% vit C, 33% folate.

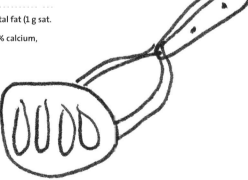

BAKED BUTTERNUT SQUASH PURÉE

The richness of squash subtly sweetened with apple makes this smooth dish a winner. Try it with other winter squash, such as sweet dumpling, buttercup, delicata or small hubbard.

Makes 4 to 6 servings

1	butternut squash (about 2 lb/1 kg)	1
¾ tsp	ground cumin	4 mL
¼ tsp	each salt and pepper	1 mL
1	apple	1
3 tbsp	chicken or vegetable stock	50 mL
1 tbsp	extra-virgin olive oil	15 mL

↙ Cut squash in half lengthwise; scoop out seeds. In small bowl, mix together ½ tsp (2 mL) of the cumin, salt and pepper; sprinkle half over squash. Halve and core apple; sprinkle with remaining cumin mixture. Place squash and apple, cut side down, in greased glass baking dish; bake in 425°F (220°C) oven until squash is tender, about 45 minutes.

↙ Peel squash and apple; place in bowl and mash together. Stir in stock, oil and remaining cumin.

PER EACH OF 6 SERVINGS: about 84 cal, 1 g pro, 3 g total fat (trace sat. fat), 16 g carb, 3 g fibre, 0 mg chol, 125 mg sodium. % RDI: 5% calcium, 7% iron, 87% vit A, 32% vit C, 11% folate.

ROAST SQUASH

↤153

When squash is plentiful, you'll want to include it in meals as often as possible.

Makes 4 servings

1	acorn squash (2 lb/1 kg)	1
2 tbsp	extra-virgin olive oil	25 mL
½ tsp	each salt and dried thyme	2 mL
Pinch	pepper	Pinch

↙ Cut squash in half lengthwise; scoop out seeds. Cut crosswise into ½-inch (1 cm) thick slices; place on rimmed baking sheet.

↙ Combine oil, salt, thyme and pepper; brush over squash. Roast in 425°F (220°C) oven until tender, about 25 minutes.

PER SERVING: about 130 cal, 1 g pro, 7 g total fat (1 g sat. fat), 18 g carb, 2 g fibre, 0 mg chol, 292 mg sodium. % RDI: 5% calcium, 9% iron, 6% vit A, 23% vit C, 11% folate.

BAKED POTATO SKINS

154 →

This favourite pub grub is always welcome. The selection of toppings gives family and guests lots of nibbling options.

Makes 8 servings

6	large baking potatoes (about 4 lb/2 kg)	6
¼ tsp	each salt and pepper	1 mL
1 cup	shredded Cheddar, Swiss or Asiago cheese	250 mL

TOPPINGS

8	slices bacon, cooked and crumbled	8
4	plum tomatoes, chopped	4
3	green onions, chopped	3
½ cup	chopped drained oil-packed sun-dried tomatoes	125 mL
½ cup	pesto or chopped pitted olives	125 mL
½ cup	light sour cream	125 mL

← Scrub potatoes; prick several times with fork. Bake in 450°F (230°C) oven until tender, about 1 hour. Let stand until cool enough to handle. *Make-ahead: Let cool completely; refrigerate in airtight container for up to 2 days.*

← Cut lengthwise in half; scoop out flesh, leaving ½-inch (1 cm) thick walls (reserve flesh for another use, such as soup or mashed potatoes). Cut each half lengthwise in half. Arrange, cut side up, on rimmed baking sheet; sprinkle with salt and pepper, then cheese. *Make-ahead: Cover and refrigerate for up to 2 hours; add a few minutes to baking time.* Bake in 450°F (230°C) oven until cheese melts, about 10 minutes.

← **TOPPINGS:** Place bacon, plum tomatoes, onions, sun-dried tomatoes, pesto and sour cream in separate small bowls to serve with potato skins.

PER SERVING: about 312 cal, 11 g pro, 16 g total fat (7 g sat. fat), 33 g carb, 5 g fibre, 28 mg chol, 454 mg sodium. % RDI: 18% calcium, 24% iron, 11% vit A, 45% vit C, 13% folate.

LEMON HERB CORN

There's no muss or fuss when using frozen corn.

Makes 4 servings

1 tbsp	butter or vegetable oil	**15 mL**
3 cups	frozen corn	**750 mL**
¼ tsp	each salt and pepper	**1 mL**
FLAVOURINGS		
1 tbsp	chopped fresh parsley	**15 mL**
1 tsp	grated lemon rind	**5 mL**
½ tsp	dried thyme	**2 mL**

⬅ In saucepan, heat butter over medium heat. Add corn, salt and pepper; cover and cook, stirring occasionally, until steaming, about 6 minutes.
⬅ **FLAVOURINGS:** Mix in parsley, lemon rind and thyme.

PER SERVING: about 121 cal, 3 g pro, 3 g total fat (2 g sat. fat), 23 g carb, 2 g fibre, 9 mg chol, 179 mg sodium. % RDI: 1% calcium, 4% iron, 6% vit A, 8% vit C, 17% folate.

VARIATIONS

CORN AND TOMATO
Omit flavourings. Substitute 1 tomato, chopped, 1 tbsp (15 mL) chopped fresh parsley and 1 tsp (5 mL) dried oregano.

CORIANDER CORN
Omit flavourings. Substitute 1 tbsp (15 mL) chopped fresh coriander, 1 tsp (5 mL) grated lime rind, 2 tsp (10 mL) lime juice and 2 cloves garlic, minced.

GOLDEN MASHED POTATO CASSEROLE

Make any special-occasion meal a little easier by preparing this dish a day ahead. Just pop it into the oven to reheat while dinner cooks.

Makes 8 to 10 servings

10	Yukon Gold potatoes (about 3½ lb/1.75 kg)	**10**
½ cup	chopped fresh chives or green onions	**125 mL**
½ cup	milk, heated	**125 mL**
½ cup	herbed cream cheese	**125 mL**
2 tbsp	butter	**25 mL**
1	egg, lightly beaten	**1**
½ tsp	each salt and pepper	**2 mL**
⅓ cup	shredded old Cheddar cheese	**75 mL**

⬅ Peel and cut potatoes into chunks. In large pot of boiling salted water, cover and cook potatoes until tender, about 20 minutes; drain and return to pot. Add ⅓ cup (75 mL) of the chives, the milk, cream cheese, butter, egg, salt and pepper; mash together until smooth.
⬅ Spoon into greased 8-inch (2 L) square glass baking dish. Sprinkle with Cheddar cheese and remaining chives. *Make-ahead: Let cool for 30 minutes. Refrigerate until cool; cover and refrigerate for up to 24 hours. Uncover. Increase baking time to 55 minutes.*
⬅ Bake in 375°F (190°C) oven until knife inserted in centre comes out hot, about 40 minutes.

PER EACH OF 10 SERVINGS: about 190 cal, 5 g pro, 8 g total fat (5 g sat. fat), 24 g carb, 2 g fibre, 45 mg chol, 488 mg sodium. % RDI: 6% calcium, 5% iron, 11% vit A, 17% vit C, 7% folate.

CHAPTER 6

MEAT A
POULTR

NDY

⬅ 161

SAUCY CAJUN ROUND STEAK

Less-tender cuts of meat, such as this marinating steak, are not only inexpensive but also lean and high in protein and iron. You can use a pressure cooker to speed things up, a slow cooker to slow things down, or simply simmer it on the stove top. Lovely with mashed potatoes and corn.

Makes 4 servings

¼ cup	all-purpose flour	50 mL
¼ tsp	each salt and pepper	1 mL
1 lb	inside round marinating steak	500 g
1 tbsp	vegetable oil	15 mL
2	strips bacon, chopped	2
2	onions, sliced	2
2	cloves garlic, minced	2
2	stalks celery, sliced	2
2 tsp	Cajun seasoning	10 mL
1 tsp	dried thyme	5 mL
¼ cup	tomato paste	50 mL
1½ cups	beef stock	375 mL
1	sweet green pepper, chopped	1
2	green onions, chopped	2
2 tbsp	chopped fresh parsley	25 mL

← In large plastic bag, shake together flour, salt and pepper. Cut steak into 8 pieces. One piece at a time, seal steak in bag; pound with flat side of meat mallet to ¼-inch (5 mm) thickness, working flour mixture into meat. Reserve any remaining flour mixture.

← In Dutch oven, heat oil over medium-high heat; brown meat well, in batches. Remove to plate.

← Add bacon to pan; cook over medium heat until crisp, about 5 minutes. Drain off fat. Add onions, garlic, celery, Cajun seasoning and thyme; cook, stirring, until onions are softened, about 5 minutes.

← Sprinkle with any reserved flour mixture; cook, stirring, for 1 minute. Whisk tomato paste into stock; pour into pan, stirring and scraping up brown bits from bottom of pan. Return steaks and any accumulated juices to pan.

← Cover and simmer over low heat, turning steaks halfway through, for 1 hour and 45 minutes. Add green pepper. Simmer, covered, until steaks are fork-tender and green pepper is tender-crisp, about 15 minutes. Sprinkle with green onions and parsley.

PER SERVING: about 310 cal, 31 g pro, 13 g total fat (4 g sat. fat), 18 g carb, 3 g fibre, 55 mg chol, 630 mg sodium. % RDI: 5% calcium, 30% iron, 11% vit A, 60% vit C, 20% folate.

SLOW COOKER SAUCY CAJUN ROUND STEAK

← Follow first paragraph as directed. In skillet, brown meat; transfer to slow cooker. Whisk tomato paste into 2 cups (500 mL) beef stock; pour into skillet and bring to boil, scraping up brown bits. Pour into slow cooker.

← Add remaining ingredients, except green pepper, green onions and parsley. Cover and cook, stirring twice, until meat is tender: on low for 8 hours or on high for 4 to 6 hours. Add green pepper; cook on high for 15 minutes. Serve sprinkled with green onions and parsley.

PRESSURE COOKER SAUCY CAJUN ROUND STEAK

← Increase stock to 2 cups (500 mL). Using pressure cooker instead of Dutch oven, follow first 3 paragraphs.

← Secure lid; bring to high pressure over high heat. Reduce heat to maintain high pressure; cook for 15 minutes. Remove from heat; let pressure release completely, about 10 minutes. Stir in green pepper; simmer, uncovered, until tender-crisp, about 10 minutes. Serve sprinkled with green onions and parsley.

PEPPERCORN STEAK WITH SWEET POTATO MASH AND GINGER SAUCE

Fresh ginger zips up a quick little sauce. We like to serve it with sautéed rapini for its mild bitterness, an appealing contrast to the sweet potatoes.

Makes 4 servings

4	strip loin or rib eye grilling steaks (about 1½ lb/750 g)	4
3 tbsp	vegetable oil	50 mL
2 tsp	cracked peppercorns	10 mL
1 tsp	Dijon mustard	5 mL
½ tsp	ground coriander (optional)	2 mL
½ tsp	salt	2 mL
Half	onion, finely chopped	Half
2	cloves garlic, minced	2
½ cup	dry white wine or chicken stock	125 mL
¼ cup	chicken or beef stock	50 mL
2 tbsp	butter	25 mL
1 tbsp	minced gingerroot	15 mL
2 tbsp	chopped fresh chives or green onions	25 mL

SWEET POTATO MASH

2	large sweet potatoes (2 lb/1 kg), peeled and cubed	2
¼ cup	butter	50 mL
½ tsp	each salt and pepper	2 mL

←167

SWEET POTATO MASH: In large pot of boiling salted water, cook potatoes until tender, about 20 minutes. Drain and return to pot. Using potato masher, mash together potatoes, butter, salt and pepper until smooth. *Make-ahead: Let cool. Refrigerate in airtight container for up to 24 hours; reheat over low heat.*

Meanwhile, trim visible fat from steaks. In small bowl, combine 1 tbsp (15 mL) of the oil, peppercorns, mustard, coriander (if using) and salt; rub over steaks to coat evenly. *Make-ahead: Cover and refrigerate for up to 1 hour.*

In large ovenproof skillet, heat 1 tbsp (15 mL) of the remaining oil over medium-high heat; brown steaks on 1 side. Turn and cook until medium-rare, about 8 minutes, or desired doneness. Transfer to cutting board; tent with foil and let stand for 5 minutes.

Meanwhile, in same pan, heat remaining oil over medium heat; fry onion and garlic, stirring occasionally, until light golden, about 3 minutes.

Add wine and stock; bring to boil. Boil, stirring and scraping up brown bits from pan, until reduced slightly. Whisk in butter and ginger. Serve with steak and mashed potatoes. Sprinkle with chives.

PER SERVING: about 735 cal, 43 g pro, 38 g total fat (15 g sat. fat), 52 g carb, 6 g fibre, 123 mg chol, 1,482 mg sodium. % RDI: 7% calcium, 34% iron, 357% vit A, 52% vit C, 16% folate.

GROUND BEEF CURRY

168 →

With a foundation of authentic Indian curry paste (as mild or hot as you wish), this dish is ready in less than 30 minutes. Long-grain rice, such as basmati with its nutty aroma and flavour, is the accompaniment we like best.

Makes 4 servings

1 lb	lean ground beef	**500 g**
1 tbsp	vegetable oil	**15 mL**
1	onion, chopped	**1**
1	jalapeño pepper, seeded and minced (optional)	**1**
¼ cup	mild Indian curry paste	**50 mL**
1	can (28 oz/796 mL) diced tomatoes	**1**
2	potatoes, diced	**2**
½ tsp	salt	**2 mL**
1 cup	frozen peas	**250 mL**
¼ cup	chopped fresh coriander	**50 mL**
1 tbsp	chopped fresh mint (or 2 tsp/10 mL dried)	**15 mL**

← In large nonstick skillet, sauté beef over medium-high heat, breaking up with spoon, until no longer pink, about 5 minutes. With slotted spoon, transfer beef to bowl. Drain fat from pan.

← Add oil to pan; fry onion, and jalapeño pepper (if using) until golden, about 4 minutes. Add curry paste; cook, stirring, until fragrant, about 1 minute.

← Stir in beef, tomatoes, potatoes and salt; cover and simmer until potatoes are tender, about 15 minutes.

← Add peas, half of the coriander and the mint; heat through. Sprinkle with remaining coriander.

PER SERVING: about 436 cal, 28 g pro, 23 g total fat (5 g sat. fat), 31 g carb, 5 g fibre, 60 mg chol, 1,104 mg sodium. % RDI: 8% calcium, 30% iron, 14% vit A, 62% vit C, 18% folate.

RAITA

← 169

Raita is a yogurt salad offered as a cooling condiment with many curries. Plain Balkan-style yogurt has the best taste and consistency for this raita. You can substitute 1 can (14 oz/398 mL) beets, drained and chopped, for the cucumber.

Makes about 2 cups (500 mL)

2 cups	plain yogurt	**500 mL**
1 cup	grated cucumber or radishes	**250 mL**
2 tbsp	minced fresh mint	**25 mL**
Pinch	cayenne pepper	**Pinch**

← In fine sieve set over bowl, drain yogurt for 20 minutes; discard liquid. In small bowl, mix together yogurt, cucumber, mint and cayenne pepper.

PER ¼ CUP (50 mL): about 37 cal, 3 g pro, 2 g total fat (1 g sat. fat), 3 g carb, trace fibre, 5 mg chol, 209 mg sodium. % RDI: 8% calcium, 1% iron, 2% vit A, 2% vit C, 4% folate.

CHILI WITH FETA IN TORTILLA SHELLS

Chili may be old hat, so it needs a bit of a surprise. That's where the olives and feta come in — and why it's served in crunchy baked tortilla shells.

Makes 4 to 6 servings

1 lb	lean ground beef	500 g
1	onion, chopped	1
1	zucchini, cubed	1
1	sweet green pepper, chopped	1
2	cloves garlic, minced	2
1 tsp	dried oregano	5 mL
¼ tsp	each salt and pepper	1 mL
1	can (19 oz/540 mL) white or red kidney beans, drained and rinsed	1
1	can (28 oz/796 mL) crushed tomatoes	1
½ cup	black olives, pitted and chopped	125 mL
	Baked Tortilla Shells (recipe, this page)	
½ cup	crumbled feta cheese	125 mL
2 tbsp	minced fresh parsley	25 mL

← In Dutch oven, fry beef over medium-high heat, breaking up with spoon, until no longer pink, about 5 minutes. Drain off fat.

← Add onion, zucchini, green pepper, garlic, oregano, salt and pepper; fry over medium heat, stirring occasionally, until onion is softened, about 4 minutes.

← Add kidney beans and tomatoes; bring to boil. Reduce heat, cover and simmer until chili is thickened, about 20 minutes.

← Stir in olives. Serve in tortilla shells; sprinkle with feta and parsley.

←171

PER EACH OF 6 SERVINGS: about 587 cal, 31 g pro, 22 g total fat (7 g sat. fat), 69 g carb, 11 g fibre, 51 mg chol, 865 mg sodium. % RDI: 18% calcium, 56% iron, 13% vit A, 50% vit C, 62% folate.

BAKED TORTILLA SHELLS

Makes 6 servings

6	large tortillas	6
2 tbsp	vegetable oil	25 mL
½ tsp	each salt and pepper	2 mL

← Brush both sides of tortillas with oil; sprinkle with salt and pepper. Press into 1-cup (250 mL) custard or muffin cups. Bake in 400°F (200°C) oven until crisp, about 7 minutes.

PER SERVING: about 225 cal, 5 g pro, 9 g total fat (1 g sat. fat), 32 g carb, 2 g fibre, 0 mg chol, 462 mg sodium. % RDI: 2% calcium, 14% iron, 32% folate.

LIGHTENED-UP SALSA MEAT LOAF

Nothing says comfort food more than a thick slice of meat loaf served with mashed potatoes and gravy. This lean version of the old-fashioned favourite uses extra-lean ground beef with rolled oats and vegetables to increase the fibre. A salsa topping instead of the usual high-sugar ketchup or chili sauce contributes fewer calories. Cooking the loaf on a baking sheet also allows the fat to drain away.

Makes 8 servings

4	egg whites	4
1 cup	large-flake rolled oats	250 mL
1	onion, grated	1
1 cup	grated zucchini	250 mL
¾ cup	grated carrot	175 mL
4	cloves garlic, minced	4
1 tsp	Worcestershire sauce	5 mL
¾ tsp	salt	4 mL
½ tsp	each dried thyme and pepper	2 mL
1½ lb	extra-lean ground beef	750 g
½ cup	salsa	125 mL

← In bowl, lightly whisk egg whites; stir in oats, onion, zucchini, carrot, garlic, Worcestershire sauce, salt, thyme and pepper. Mix in beef.

← Place on greased rimmed baking sheet; form into 13-inch (33 cm) long by 2-inch (5 cm) high oval loaf. Bake in 350°F (180°C) oven until browned, about 40 minutes.

← Spread salsa over top; bake until meat thermometer inserted in centre registers 160°F (71°C), about 20 minutes.

←173

PER SERVING: about 206 cal, 22 g pro, 7 g total fat (3 g sat. fat), 12 g carb, 2 g fibre, 47 mg chol, 382 mg sodium. % RDI: 3% calcium, 19% iron, 25% vit A, 7% vit C, 7% folate.

PAN-FRIED SIRLOIN STEAK WITH MUSHROOMS AND ONIONS

A cast-iron skillet is the way to go when pan-frying steak.

Makes 4 servings

3	cloves garlic, minced	3
½ tsp	salt	2 mL
4 tsp	vegetable oil	20 mL
¾ tsp	pepper	4 mL
1 lb	thick-cut top sirloin grilling steak	500 g
2	onions, thinly sliced	2
3 cups	button mushrooms	750 mL
1 tbsp	all-purpose flour	15 mL
½ cup	beef stock	125 mL
1 tbsp	wine vinegar	15 mL
1 tbsp	minced fresh parsley	15 mL

← In small bowl and with back of spoon or fork, mash garlic with half of the salt until smooth as paste; mix in 1 tsp (5 mL) of the oil and pepper. Rub onto both sides of steak; let stand for 10 minutes.

← Heat large skillet over high heat until almost smoking. Fry steak, turning once, until medium-rare, 12 to 14 minutes. Transfer to cutting board and tent with foil; let stand for about 5 minutes before slicing thinly on the diagonal.

← Meanwhile, in same skillet, heat remaining oil over medium-high heat; sauté onions until softened, about 2 minutes.

← Add mushrooms and remaining salt; sauté, stirring often, until golden, 5 minutes. Sprinkle with flour, stirring to coat mushroom mixture.

← Add stock and vinegar; bring to boil and boil until thickened, about 1 minute. Sprinkle with parsley. Serve with steak.

PER SERVING: about 228 cal, 26 g pro, 9 g total fat (2 g sat. fat), 9 g carb, 2 g fibre, 54 mg chol, 458 mg sodium. % RDI: 4% calcium, 26% iron, 1% vit A, 10% vit C, 12% folate.

MAKE-YOUR-OWN TACOS

This kid-tested supper eliminates busy-day burnout. Set out individual bowls of lettuce, tomatoes and cheese, so the kids can assemble their own tacos.

Makes 4 servings

12 oz	lean ground beef	**375 g**
1	onion, chopped	**1**
1 tbsp	chili powder	**15 mL**
1 tsp	dried oregano	**5 mL**
1	can (19 oz/540 mL) red kidney beans, drained and rinsed	**1**
1¾ cups	mild salsa	**425 mL**
12	taco shells or small flour tortillas	**12**
1 cup	shredded lettuce	**250 mL**
1 cup	chopped tomatoes	**250 mL**
1 cup	shredded cheese	**250 mL**

←177

← In large nonstick skillet, fry beef over medium-high heat, breaking up with spoon, until no longer pink, about 5 minutes. With slotted spoon, transfer to bowl; drain fat from pan.

← Add onion, chili powder and oregano to pan; fry over medium heat, stirring occasionally, until softened about 5 minutes.

← Add beef, beans and salsa; simmer for 5 minutes. Divide among taco shells. Top with lettuce, tomatoes and cheese.

PER SERVING: about 609 cal, 36 g pro, 28 g total fat (9 g sat. fat), 55 g carb, 14 g fibre, 72 mg chol, 851 mg sodium. % RDI: 34% calcium, 36% iron, 26% vit A, 58% vit C, 40% folate.

TIP

You can also use ground pork, veal or sausage instead of the beef.

CHEESEBURGER PIZZA

When the pizza comes out of the oven, you can add some cheeseburger-inspired toppings. How about pickled hot peppers, diced tomatoes and shredded lettuce for that irresistible taste factor?

Makes 4 servings

8 oz	lean ground beef	250 g
1	small onion, chopped	1
3	cloves garlic, minced	3
½ tsp	dried oregano	2 mL
¼ tsp	each salt and pepper	1 mL
1 lb	pizza dough	500 g
¼ cup	pizza sauce or pasta sauce	50 mL
¾ cup	each shredded Cheddar and mozzarella cheese	175 mL

← In skillet, fry beef, onion, garlic, oregano, salt and pepper over medium-high heat, breaking up with spoon, until beef is no longer pink, about 5 minutes. Drain off fat. Set aside.

←179

← On lightly floured surface, roll out dough into 12-inch (30 cm) circle, letting dough rest if too elastic to roll. Centre on greased 12-inch (30 cm) pizza pan.

← Spread pizza sauce over dough. Top evenly with beef mixture. Sprinkle with Cheddar and mozzarella cheeses. Bake on lowest rack position in 500°F (260°C) oven until cheese is bubbly and crust is golden and slightly puffed, about 10 minutes.

PER SERVING: about 594 cal, 30 g pro, 26 g total fat (12 g sat. fat), 59 g carb, 2 g fibre, 80 mg chol, 1,041 mg sodium. % RDI: 30% calcium, 29% iron, 14% vit A, 3% vit C, 21% folate.

BEEF CALZONE

While making the filling for calzone, why not double the amount and freeze half for another fuss-free supper?

Makes 4 servings

8 oz	lean ground beef	**250 g**
1	small onion, chopped	**1**
2	cloves garlic, minced	**2**
1	small sweet green pepper, sliced	**1**
1 cup	sliced mushrooms	**250 mL**
1 tsp	dried basil	**5 mL**
¼ tsp	each salt and pepper	**1 mL**
1	carrot, grated	**1**
¾ cup	tomato sauce	**175 mL**
1 lb	pizza dough	**500 g**
1 cup	shredded mozzarella or Monterey Jack cheese	**250 mL**
2 tbsp	cornmeal	**25 mL**
1 tbsp	all-purpose flour	**15 mL**

← In skillet, fry beef over medium-high heat, breaking up with spoon, until no longer pink, about 5 minutes. Drain off fat.

← Add onion, garlic, green pepper, mushrooms, basil, salt and pepper; fry, stirring occasionally, until onion is softened, about 5 minutes. Stir in carrot and tomato sauce; set aside.

← Divide dough into quarters; shape each into disc. On lightly floured surface, roll out each disc into 8-inch (20 cm) circle. Divide filling over half of each circle; sprinkle with cheese. Fold dough over; pinch or press firmly with fork to seal. *Make-ahead: Freeze on parchment paper–lined rimmed baking sheet; transfer to airtight container and freeze for up to 2 weeks. Thaw in refrigerator.*

← Sprinkle rimmed baking sheet with cornmeal. Place calzones on top; dust with flour. Bake in centre of 425°F (220°C) oven until golden, about 20 minutes.

PER SERVING: about 559 cal, 27 g pro, 19 g total fat (8 g sat. fat), 70 g carb, 4 g fibre, 58 mg chol, 1,127 mg sodium. % RDI: 21% calcium, 34% iron, 59% vit A, 35% vit C, 26% folate.

COCONUT CURRY MEATBALLS

Everyday meatballs pick up the trendy flavour of Thai coconut sauce. Serve with noodles or rice and sprinkle with chopped fresh coriander.

Makes 4 servings

1	onion, finely chopped	1
1	clove garlic, minced	1
1	can (400 mL) coconut milk	1
1 cup	chicken stock	250 mL
2 tbsp	lime juice	25 mL
1	sweet red pepper, chopped	1
1 tbsp	red or yellow mild Thai or Indian curry paste	15 mL

MEATBALLS

⅔ cup	fresh bread crumbs	150 mL
1	egg	1
1	clove garlic, minced	1
½ tsp	each salt and pepper	2 mL
1 lb	lean ground beef	500 g
¼ cup	chopped fresh coriander	50 mL
2 tbsp	minced gingerroot	25 mL

← **MEATBALLS:** In bowl, combine bread crumbs with ½ cup (125 mL) water; let stand until absorbed, about 5 minutes. Beat in egg, garlic, salt and pepper. Add beef, coriander and ginger; mix well. Roll by rounded 1 tbsp (15 mL) into balls. *Make-ahead: Freeze in layers separated by waxed paper; transfer to airtight container and freeze for up to 1 month.*

← In large nonstick skillet, brown meatballs, in batches, over medium-high heat; transfer to bowl. Drain off fat.

← Add onion and garlic to pan; fry over medium heat, stirring often, for 3 minutes. Add coconut milk, chicken stock, lime juice, red pepper and curry paste; simmer, stirring occasionally, until slightly thickened, about 25 minutes.

← Return meatballs and any accumulated juices to pan; simmer, turning meatballs occasionally, until no longer pink inside and sauce is thickened, about 20 minutes.

←183

PER SERVING: about 517 cal, 29 g pro, 40 g total fat (25 g sat. fat), 13 g carb, 1 g fibre, 114 mg chol, 728 mg sodium. % RDI: 6% calcium, 44% iron, 13% vit A, 88% vit C, 20% folate.

❦

VARIATION

GOULASH MEATBALLS IN MUSHROOM SAUCE

← **MEATBALLS:** Substitute 1 tbsp (15 mL) each paprika and tomato paste for the coriander and ginger.

← Omit all other ingredients. In skillet used to brown meatballs, sauté 4 cups (1 L) sliced mushrooms, 1 onion, finely chopped, and 1 clove garlic, minced, until no liquid remains, about 6 minutes.

← Stir in 2 cups (500 mL) beef stock, 1 cup (250 mL) water, ¼ cup (50 mL) tomato paste, 2 tbsp (25 mL) paprika, and 2 tbsp (25 mL) sherry (optional). Continue with recipe.

MEATBALL SOUVLAKI

This fresh version of a familiar fast-food menu item is on the table in minutes — probably less time than it takes to order in or drive to a restaurant.

Makes 4 servings

1 cup	plain low-fat yogurt	250 mL
½ cup	grated (unpeeled) English cucumber	125 mL
1	clove garlic, minced	1
¼ tsp	dried mint	1 mL
Pinch	each salt and pepper	Pinch
4	Greek pita breads, warmed	4
2 cups	shredded lettuce	500 mL
2	small tomatoes, chopped	2
4	thin slices red onion	4
MEATBALLS		
1	egg	1
¼ cup	dry bread crumbs	50 mL
1 tbsp	Dijon mustard	15 mL
½ tsp	dried oregano	2 mL
¼ tsp	each salt and pepper	1 mL
1 lb	lean ground beef	500 g

←185

MEATBALLS: Line rimmed baking sheet with foil; grease foil. Set aside.

In bowl, whisk egg; whisk in bread crumbs, mustard, oregano, salt and pepper;. Mix in beef. Roll by heaping 1 tbsp (15 mL) into 24 balls; place on prepared pan. Bake in 450°F (230°C) oven until meat thermometer inserted into a few of the meatballs registers 160°F (71°C), about 15 minutes.

In bowl, combine yogurt, cucumber, garlic, mint, salt and pepper; spread over pitas. Sprinkle with lettuce. Divide tomatoes, onion then meatballs over half of each pita; fold remaining half over top.

PER SERVING: about 476 cal, 34 g pro, 16 g total fat (6 g sat. fat), 48 g carb, 3 g fibre. 115 mg chol, 682 mg sodium. % RDI: 19% calcium, 34% iron, 8% vit A, 20% vit C, 48% folate.

TIP

Greek pitas don't have pockets; if they're unavailable, put the filling in the pockets of regular pitas.

BEEF PATTIES WITH CHERRY TOMATO SAUCE

If you commit this fresh tomato sauce to memory, you can whip it up to serve with sautéed chicken breasts or fish fillets, too. If olives are not your favourite, just leave them out.

Makes 4 servings

1	egg	1
1	clove garlic, minced	1
1 tsp	dried oregano	5 mL
1 tsp	grated lemon rind	5 mL
¼ tsp	each salt and pepper	1 mL
1 lb	lean ground beef	500 g
CHERRY TOMATO SAUCE		
2 tsp	vegetable oil	10 mL
2	cloves garlic, minced	2
3 cups	cherry tomatoes, halved	750 mL
1 tbsp	tomato paste	15 mL
¼ tsp	each salt and pepper	1 mL
2 tbsp	sliced pitted black olives	25 mL
2 tbsp	chopped fresh parsley	25 mL

← In bowl, beat together egg, 2 tbsp (25 mL) water, garlic, oregano, lemon rind, salt and pepper; mix in beef. Shape into four ½-inch (1 cm) thick patties. *Make-ahead: Separate by waxed paper, wrap and refrigerate for up to 24 hours. Or freeze in airtight container for up to 1 month; thaw in refrigerator.*

← In nonstick skillet, fry patties over medium-high heat, turning once, until thermometer inserted sideways into centre registers 160°F (71°C), about 12 minutes. Transfer to plate; cover and keep warm. Drain off fat and wipe out pan.

← **CHERRY TOMATO SAUCE:** In same skillet, heat oil over medium heat; fry garlic and tomatoes for 2 minutes. Add ¼ cup (50 mL) water, tomato paste, salt and pepper; boil, stirring, until thickened and tomatoes are softened, about 5 minutes.

← Add olives and parsley. Serve over patties.

PER SERVING: about 250 cal, 24 g pro, 15 g total fat (5 g sat. fat), 7 g carb, 2 g fibre, 106 mg chol, 407 mg sodium. % RDI: 3% calcium, 22% iron, 10% vit A, 37% vit C, 12% folate.

THE BEST BURGER

Fire up the grill or heat the grill pan or skillet and get ready to indulge everyone — with juicy burgers. A topping of colourful sweet peppers and a fresh herb mayonnaise turns the everyday into premiere fare. You can add lettuce to the buns and top the burgers with cheese slices a few minutes before taking them off the grill.

Makes 4 servings

1	egg	1
2 tbsp	water, tomato juice, stock or red wine	25 mL
¼ cup	dry bread crumbs	50 mL
1	small onion, grated	1
1 tbsp	Dijon or hot mustard or prepared horseradish	15 mL
1	clove garlic, minced	1
½ tsp	each salt and pepper	2 mL
1 lb	lean ground beef, pork, lamb, veal, turkey or chicken	500 g
4	sesame seed hamburger buns	4

← In bowl, whisk egg with water; stir in bread crumbs, onion, mustard, garlic, salt and pepper. Mix in beef. Shape into four ¾-inch (2 cm) thick patties. *Make-ahead: Separate by waxed paper, wrap and refrigerate for up to 24 hours. Or freeze in airtight container for up to 1 month; thaw in refrigerator.*

← Place patties on greased grill over medium heat; close lid and grill, turning once, until no longer pink inside and digital thermometer inserted sideways into centre reads 160°F (71°C), about 15 minutes. Sandwich in bun.

PER SERVING: about 425 cal, 29 g pro, 17 g total fat (6 g sat. fat), 37 g carb, 2 g fibre, 108 mg chol, 807 mg sodium. % RDI: 12% calcium, 34% iron, 2% vit A, 2% vit C, 34% folate.

SAUTÉED PEPPERS

Tender-crisp peppers are like a fresh relish and a welcome change from sweet condiments.

Makes 1 cup (25 mL) or 4 servings

1 tsp	vegetable oil	5 mL
Half	each sweet red and yellow pepper, thinly sliced	Half
2	cloves garlic, minced	2
¼ tsp	hot pepper flakes (optional)	1 mL
¼ cup	minced fresh coriander or parsley	50 mL
2 tbsp	dry white wine (or 1 tsp/5 mL vinegar)	25 mL
1 tbsp	tomato paste	15 mL
¼ tsp	salt	1 mL

← In skillet, heat oil over medium heat; fry red and yellow peppers, garlic, and hot pepper flakes (if using) until peppers are tender-crisp, about 5 minutes.

← Stir in coriander, wine, tomato paste and salt; cook until liquid is evaporated, about 3 minutes.

PER SERVING: about 28 cal, 1 g pro, 1 g total fat (trace g sat. fat), 3 g carb, 1 g fibre, 0 mg chol, 147 mg sodium. % RDI: 1% calcium, 2% iron, 7% vit A, 82% vit C, 3% folate.

FRESH HERB MAYONNAISE

Excellent with beef, pork or chicken burgers, this mayonnaise is also a fine topping for grilled or roasted fish.

← 189

Makes ⅓ cup (75 mL) or 4 servings

3 tbsp	light mayonnaise	50 mL
1 tbsp	each minced fresh basil, parsley and chives	15 mL
1 tbsp	extra-virgin olive oil (optional)	15 mL
1	small clove garlic, minced	1
1 tsp	lemon juice	5 mL
1 tsp	Dijon mustard	5 mL
Dash	hot pepper sauce	Dash

← In bowl, mix together mayonnaise, basil, parsley, chives, oil (if using), garlic, lemon juice, mustard and hot pepper sauce.

PER SERVING: about 38 cal, trace pro, 4 g total fat (1 g sat. fat), 1 g carb, trace fibre, 4 mg chol, 100 mg sodium. % RDI: 1% calcium, 1% iron, 1% vit A, 3% vit C, 1% folate.

MOUSSAKA

This casserole of layered eggplant, tomato-and-beef sauce with a custard topping of feta and cottage cheese is family friendly and perfect to make ahead or freeze. It's high on the list of perfect potluck dishes.

Makes 8 servings

2	eggplants (2½ lb/1.25 kg)	**2**
1 tbsp	salt	**15 mL**
2 tbsp	extra-virgin olive oil	**25 mL**
½ cup	fresh bread crumbs	**125 mL**
¼ cup	grated Parmesan cheese	**50 mL**

MEAT SAUCE

2 lb	lean ground beef or lamb	**1 kg**
2	onions, chopped	**2**
4	cloves garlic, minced	**4**
1 tbsp	dried oregano	**15 mL**
1 tsp	cinnamon	**5 mL**
¼ tsp	pepper	**1 mL**
1 cup	red wine	**250 mL**
1	can (19 oz/540 mL) tomatoes	**1**
1	can (5½ oz/156 mL) tomato paste	**1**
½ cup	chopped fresh parsley	**125 mL**

CHEESE SAUCE

¼ cup	butter	**50 mL**
¼ cup	all-purpose flour	**50 mL**
2 cups	milk	**500 mL**
½ tsp	salt	**2 mL**
¼ tsp	each nutmeg and pepper	**1 mL**
1 cup	crumbled feta cheese	**250 mL**
4	eggs, beaten	**4**
2 cups	pressed dry cottage cheese	**500 mL**

← Cut eggplants into ¼-inch (5 mm) thick slices; layer in colander, sprinkling each layer with salt. Let stand for 30 minutes.

← **MEAT SAUCE:** Meanwhile, in large skillet, fry beef over high heat, breaking up with spoon, until no longer pink, about 5 minutes. Drain off fat. Add onions, garlic, oregano, cinnamon and pepper; sauté over medium-high heat until onions are softened, about 5 minutes.

← Add wine, tomatoes and tomato paste, breaking up tomatoes with spoon; bring to boil. Reduce heat to medium; cook until mixture does not fill in when spoon is drawn through pan, about 10 minutes. Stir in parsley. Set aside.

← Rinse eggplant; drain well and pat dry. In batches, brush eggplant with oil and broil on baking sheet, turning once, until golden and translucent, 8 to 12 minutes. Set aside.

← **CHEESE SAUCE:** In saucepan, melt butter over medium heat; whisk in flour and cook, whisking, for 2 minutes, without browning. Gradually whisk in milk and cook until boiling and thickened enough to coat back of spoon, about 5 minutes. Season with salt, nutmeg and pepper. Let stand for 10 minutes to cool slightly, stirring occasionally.

← Rinse feta under cold water; drain well. In large bowl, whisk together feta, eggs and cottage cheese; whisk in cheese sauce.

← Spread half of the meat sauce in 13- x 9-inch (3 L) glass baking dish. Spoon ½ cup (125 mL) of the cheese sauce on top, spreading evenly. Layer with half of the eggplant, overlapping if necessary. Repeat layers once. Pour remaining cheese sauce over top. *Make-ahead: Let cool for 30 minutes. Refrigerate until cold; cover with plastic wrap and refrigerate for up to 24 hours. Or overwrap with foil and freeze for up to 3 weeks; thaw in refrigerator for 48 hours before continuing.*

← Combine bread crumbs with Parmesan cheese; sprinkle over casserole. Bake in 350°F (180°C) oven until browned and bubbly, 1 hour and 10 minutes. Let stand for 15 minutes; cut into squares.

PER SERVING: about 565 cal, 43 g pro, 30 g total fat (14 g sat. fat), 29 g carb, 6 g fibre, 203 mg chol, 710 mg sodium. % RDI: 26% calcium, 36% iron, 28% vit A, 37% vit C, 34% folate.

PESTO BEEF KABOBS

Marinate and barbecue these right away, or marinate ahead of time so you're ready for supper any night of the week. Enjoy them with Warm Zucchini Ribbons (recipe, this page) and crunchy flatbread.

Makes 4 servings

1 lb	top sirloin grilling steak	500 g
⅓ cup	prepared pesto	75 mL
2 tbsp	extra-virgin olive oil	25 mL
1 tbsp	wine vinegar	15 mL
2	cloves garlic, minced	2

← Cut steak into 1-inch (2.5 cm) cubes. In large bowl, mix together pesto, oil, vinegar and garlic. Add beef and toss to coat; marinate for 10 minutes. *Make-ahead: Cover and refrigerate for up to 24 hours.*
← Reserving marinade, thread beef onto 8 skewers. Place on greased grill over medium-high heat; close lid and grill, brushing with remaining marinade and turning once, until medium-rare, about 8 minutes, or desired doneness.

PER SERVING: about 276 cal, 23 g pro, 20 g total fat (5 g sat. fat), 2 g carb, trace fibre, 59 mg chol, 238 mg sodium. % RDI: 7% calcium, 20% iron, 3% vit A, 3% vit C, 5% folate.

WARM ZUCCHINI RIBBONS

←193

Zucchini can be boring but not when coated in a vinaigrette, warmed and then tossed with cherry tomatoes.

Makes 4 servings

3	zucchini (1 lb/500 g)	3
2 tbsp	extra-virgin olive oil	25 mL
1 tbsp	wine vinegar	15 mL
½ tsp	dried oregano	2 mL
¼ tsp	each salt and pepper	1 mL
2 cups	cherry tomatoes, quartered	500 mL
¼ cup	toasted pine nuts (optional)	50 mL

← Using vegetable peeler or mandoline, cut zucchini into ribbon-thin slices; place in large bowl. Add oil, vinegar, oregano, salt and pepper; toss to coat. Transfer to grill basket.
← Place on grill over medium-high heat; close lid and grill until softened, 3 to 5 minutes. Return to bowl. Add tomatoes, and pine nuts (if using); toss to combine.

PER SERVING: about 89 cal, 1 g pro, 7 g total fat (1 g sat. fat), 7 g carb, 2 g fibre, 0 mg chol, 152 mg sodium. % RDI: 2% calcium, 5% iron, 6% vit A, 27% vit C, 11% folate.

WEEKNIGHT QUICK ROAST

Roasting is quick with specialty-cut small roasts, such as this one that's served with an oven-caramelized onion sauce. Check the meat counter and ask for these roasts if they are not available for pickup.

Makes 4 servings

2 tbsp	vegetable oil	25 mL
3 cups	thinly sliced onions	750 mL
4	cloves garlic, minced	4
1 tbsp	dried Italian herb seasoning	15 mL
¼ tsp	each salt and pepper	1 mL
1	sirloin tip quick roast (about 1 lb/500 g)	1
1 tbsp	all-purpose flour	15 mL
1 cup	beef stock	250 mL
4	oil-packed sun-dried tomatoes, slivered	4
1 tsp	wine vinegar	5 mL

← In ovenproof skillet, heat 1 tbsp (15 mL) of the oil over medium heat; fry onions and all but 1 tsp (5 mL) of the garlic, stirring occasionally, until light golden, about 10 minutes.

← Meanwhile, combine remaining oil and garlic, herb seasoning, salt and pepper; rub all over roast. Place on onions; roast in 350°F (180°C) oven until meat thermometer registers 155°F (68°C), about 50 minutes. Transfer roast to cutting board; tent with foil and let stand for 10 minutes for temperature to rise 5°F (3°C) for medium. Slice thinly.

← Meanwhile, sprinkle flour over onions; cook over medium heat for 1 minute. Whisk in beef stock and tomatoes; bring to boil. Reduce heat and simmer until thickened, about 5 minutes. Add vinegar. Serve with roast.

PER SERVING: about 306 cal, 28 g pro, 17 g total fat (4 g sat. fat), 11 g carb, 2 g fibre, 59 mg chol, 424 mg sodium. % RDI: 4% calcium, 23% iron, 1% vit A, 13% vit C, 10% folate.

HOISIN PORK RIBS

These sticky, crispy-edged meaty ribs are ideal for snack food or even a main course. But you'd better make plenty because they disappear all too soon.

Makes about 16 pieces

3 lb	pork side or back ribs, centre cut removed	1.5 kg
½ cup	hoisin sauce	125 mL
2 tbsp	rice vinegar	25 mL
1 tbsp	liquid honey	15 mL
4	cloves garlic, minced	4
1 tbsp	minced gingerroot	15 mL
½ tsp	hot pepper flakes	2 mL
1 tbsp	toasted sesame seeds	15 mL
2	green onions, thinly sliced	2

←197

← Pour enough water into shallow roasting pan to come about ½ inch (1 cm) up side. Cut ribs into 2-rib portions; place, meaty side up, in single layer in water. Cover and roast in 325°F (160°C) oven until meat is tender, 75 to 90 minutes; drain. *Make-ahead: Let cool; cover and refrigerate for up to 24 hours.*

← In bowl, combine hoisin sauce, vinegar, honey, garlic, ginger and hot pepper flakes. Arrange ribs on foil-lined rimmed baking sheet; brush with half of the sauce. Roast in 425°F (220°C) oven for 7 minutes.

← Brush with remaining sauce; roast until browned and slightly caramelized, about 7 minutes. Sprinkle with sesame seeds and green onions.

PER PIECE: about 160 cal, 12 g pro, 10 g total fat (3 g sat. fat), 5 g carb, trace fibre, 45 mg chol, 170 mg sodium. % RDI: 2% calcium, 7% iron, 2% vit C, 2% folate.

PORK TENDERLOIN AND BROCCOLI STIR-FRY

One pork tenderloin is just the right amount for a stir-fry supper for four, especially when combined with lots of vegetables and served over rice or quick-cooking Asian noodles. We recommend supermarket-available chow mein steamed noodles.

Makes 4 servings

1	pork tenderloin (about 12 oz/375 g)	1
1 tbsp	vegetable oil	15 mL
2	cloves garlic, minced	2
1 tbsp	minced gingerroot	15 mL
3 cups	chopped broccoli florets and peeled stems	750 mL
2	carrots, sliced	2
1	sweet red or yellow pepper, sliced	1
¾ cup	chicken stock	175 mL
½ cup	oyster sauce	125 mL
2 tbsp	soy sauce	25 mL
4 tsp	cornstarch	20 mL
1 tbsp	rice vinegar	15 mL
2	green onions, sliced	2

←199

← Slice pork in half lengthwise; cut crosswise into ½-inch (1 cm) thick slices. In large wok or skillet, heat oil over high heat; stir-fry pork until just a hint of pink remains, about 5 minutes. Transfer to plate.

← Add garlic and ginger to wok; stir-fry over medium-high heat for 30 seconds. Add broccoli, carrots, red pepper and 2 tbsp (25 mL) water; cover and steam until tender-crisp, about 3 minutes.

← Return pork and any accumulated juices to wok. Whisk together stock, oyster sauce, soy sauce, cornstarch and vinegar; stir into wok and cook, stirring, until thickened and glossy, about 1 minute. Sprinkle with green onions.

PER SERVING: about 227 cal, 25 g pro, 6 g total fat (1 g sat. fat), 18 g carb, 3 g fibre, 50 mg chol, 1,718 mg sodium. % RDI: 7% calcium, 18% iron, 112% vit A, 170% vit C, 27% folate.

PORK CHOPS PARMESAN

200 →

Serve these tomato sauce–napped chops on Parmesan Parsley Polenta (recipe, opposite) with steamed asparagus.

Makes 4 servings

⅓ cup	dry bread crumbs	75 mL
⅓ cup	grated Parmesan cheese	75 mL
1	egg	1
¼ cup	all-purpose flour	50 mL
½ tsp	crumbled dried sage	2 mL
¼ tsp	each salt and pepper	1 mL
4	pork loin centre chops boneless (total 1 lb/500 g)	4
1 tbsp	vegetable oil	15 mL
1 cup	pasta sauce	250 mL
4	slices light provolone or part-skim mozzarella cheese (4 oz/125 g)	4

← In shallow dish, mix bread crumbs with Parmesan cheese. In separate shallow dish, whisk egg. In third shallow dish, whisk together flour, sage, salt and pepper.

← Press each chop into flour mixture, turning to coat and shaking off any excess. Dip into egg, turning to coat and letting any excess drip back into dish. Press into bread crumb mixture, turning to coat.

← In large nonstick skillet, heat oil over medium-high heat; fry chops until golden and just a hint of pink remains inside, about 5 minutes per side. Transfer to 8-inch (2 L) square glass baking dish.

← Spread pasta sauce over chops; cover with cheese. Bake in 400°F (200°C) oven until bubbly and golden, about 10 minutes.

PER SERVING: about 399 cal, 42 g pro, 16 g total fat (6 g sat. fat), 18 g carb, 2 g fibre, 131 mg chol, 972 mg sodium. % RDI: 36% calcium, 19% iron, 9% vit A, 10% vit C, 14% folate.

PARMESAN PARSLEY POLENTA

You can keep cornmeal on hand without fear of it going bad. That alone has made polenta a family supper staple and a nice change from potatoes, rice or noodles.

← 201

Makes 4 servings

1 cup	cornmeal	**250 mL**
½ cup	grated Parmesan cheese	**125 mL**
¼ cup	minced fresh parsley	**50 mL**
2 tbsp	butter	**25 mL**
1 tsp	each salt and pepper	**5 mL**

← In saucepan, bring 4 cups (1 L) water to boil. In thin steady stream, whisk in cornmeal until thickened. Simmer over medium-low heat, stirring with wooden spoon, until polenta is thick enough to mound on spoon, about 10 minutes. Remove from heat.

← Stir in cheese, parsley, butter, salt and pepper.

PER SERVING: about 237 cal, 8 g pro, 10 g total fat (6 g sat. fat), 28 g carb, 2 g fibre, 28 mg chol, 875 mg sodium. % RDI: 17% calcium, 6% iron, 11% vit A, 7% vit C, 8% folate.

PORK CHOPS NIÇOISE

Pair this skillet simmer with Steamed Herb Carrots (recipe, this page) and potatoes.

Makes 4 servings

4	pork loin centre chops (about 1½ lb/750 g)	4
½ tsp	each salt and pepper	2 mL
2 tsp	vegetable oil	10 mL
1	onion, chopped	1
4	cloves garlic, minced	4
1 tsp	dried basil or herbes de Provence	5 mL
4	plum tomatoes, chopped	4
Half	large sweet green pepper, chopped	Half
½ cup	black olives	125 mL
2 tbsp	chopped fresh parsley	25 mL

← Trim any fat from chops; nick curved edge of each to prevent curling. Sprinkle with salt and pepper. In skillet, heat oil over medium-high heat; brown chops. Transfer to plate. Drain fat from pan.
← Add onion, garlic and basil to pan; fry over medium heat, stirring occasionally, until softened, about 5 minutes. Add tomatoes and green pepper; reduce heat and simmer, uncovered, for 10 minutes.
← Return chops and any accumulated juices to pan, turning to coat with sauce. Add olives; simmer until chops are tender and just a hint of pink remains inside, about 5 minutes. Serve sprinkled with parsley.

PER SERVING: about 246 cal, 25 g pro, 13 g total fat (3 g sat. fat), 9 g carb, 2 g fibre, 67 mg chol, 497 mg sodium. % RDI: 5% calcium, 16% iron, 10% vit A, 47% vit C, 8% folate.

STEAMED HERBED CARROTS

←203

Carrots are inexpensive, healthful, beautiful and take only minutes to prepare.

Makes 4 servings

4	large carrots (1 lb/500 g)	4
½ tsp	dried basil	2 mL
¼ tsp	each salt and pepper	1 mL
2 tsp	vegetable oil	10 mL

← Peel carrots; diagonally cut into ¼-inch (5 mm) thick slices. In steamer basket, toss together carrots, basil, salt and pepper; steam over saucepan of boiling water until tender-crisp, 8 to 10 minutes. Sprinkle with oil; toss to coat.

PER SERVING: about 59 cal, 1 g pro, 2 g total fat (trace sat. fat), 9 g carb, 2 g fibre, 0 mg chol, 200 mg sodium. % RDI: 3% calcium, 4% iron, 210% vit A, 3% vit C, 5% folate.

HONEY-GARLIC PORK MEDALLIONS WITH COUSCOUS

204 → When oranges, apricots and raisins combine in this quick-and-easy meal, a delicious dinner is in the offing. Bottled honey-garlic sauce saves time.

Makes 4 servings

2	pork tenderloins (each 12 oz/375 g)	2
¼ tsp	each salt and pepper	1 mL
2 tbsp	vegetable oil	25 mL
2	small navel oranges	2
1	onion, thinly sliced	1
½ cup	honey-garlic sauce	125 mL
½ cup	orange juice	125 mL
¼ cup	dried apricots	50 mL
2 tbsp	golden raisins	25 mL
1 tbsp	cornstarch	15 mL
2 tbsp	minced fresh parsley or coriander	25 mL
	Whole Wheat Couscous (recipe, opposite)	

← Cut pork into ½-inch (1 cm) thick slices; sprinkle with salt and pepper. In large skillet, heat half of the oil over medium-high heat; brown pork, in batches. Transfer to plate.

← Cut oranges into 8 wedges each. In same skillet, heat remaining oil over medium heat; fry oranges, cut side down and turning once, until browned, about 5 minutes. Add onion; fry, stirring gently, until softened and golden, about 5 minutes.

← Add honey-garlic sauce, orange juice, apricots, ¼ cup (50 mL) water and raisins; bring to boil. Cover and simmer until orange rind is fork-tender, about 5 minutes. Return pork and any accumulated juices to pan; reduce heat and simmer to blend flavours, about 5 minutes.

← Whisk cornstarch with 2 tbsp (25 mL) water; add to liquid in pan and simmer, stirring, until thickened and glossy, about 1 minute. Sprinkle with parsley. Serve with couscous.

PER SERVING: about 621 cal, 50 g pro, 16 g total fat (4 g sat. fat), 75 g carb, 9 g fibre, 100 mg chol, 721 mg sodium. % RDI: 8% calcium, 44% iron, 11% vit A, 70% vit C, 14% folate.

WHOLE WHEAT COUSCOUS

← 205

Couscous needs no cooking and is ready in minutes.

Makes 4 servings

1 tbsp	butter	15 mL
¼ tsp	salt	1 mL
1 cup	whole wheat couscous	250 mL

← In small saucepan, bring 1½ cups (375 mL) water, butter and salt to boil. Stir in couscous; remove from heat. Cover and let stand for 5 minutes. Fluff with fork.

PER SERVING: about 201 cal, 7 g pro, 4 g total fat (2 g sat. fat), 38 g carb, 6 g fibre, 9 mg chol, 175 mg sodium. % RDI: 2% calcium, 11% iron, 3% vit A.

ROAST PORK WITH SWEET POTATOES AND GARLIC

This is a superb roast to serve for family gatherings. The double loin is enough for 12 servings, so you can have eight around the table for the hot roast, vegetables and gravy, with leftovers of meat for four the next day. Roasting with convection heat cuts the time by about a quarter.

Makes 8 servings with enough pork leftover for 4 more servings

1 tsp	fennel seeds	**5 mL**
6	cloves garlic, minced	**6**
4 tsp	chopped fresh thyme (or 1 tsp/5 mL dried)	**20 mL**
1 tbsp	vegetable oil	**15 mL**
1 tsp	dry mustard	**5 mL**
½ tsp	each salt and pepper	**2 mL**
1	double pork loin centre roast boneless (about 4 lb/2 kg)	**1**

SWEET POTATOES AND GARLIC

4	sweet potatoes, peeled and halved	**4**
2	heads garlic, tips removed	**2**
2 tbsp	extra-virgin olive oil	**25 mL**
½ tsp	each salt and pepper	**2 mL**
	Fresh thyme sprigs (or ½ tsp/2 mL dried)	

GRAVY

1½ cups	chicken stock	**375 mL**
2 tbsp	all-purpose flour	**25 mL**

← Using mortar and pestle or with bottom of heavy skillet, crush fennel seeds; place in small bowl. Mix in minced garlic, thyme, oil, mustard, salt and pepper to form paste; rub all over roast. Place on rack in small roasting pan.

← **SWEET POTATOES AND GARLIC:** In bowl, toss together potatoes, garlic, oil, salt, pepper and thyme sprigs; spread on rimmed baking sheet.

← Roast pork and vegetables in 325°F (160°C) convection or conventional oven until vegetables are tender and meat thermometer inserted into centre of pork registers 160°F (70°C), about 90 minutes in convection oven or 2 hours in conventional oven. Transfer roast to cutting board; tent with foil and let stand for 10 minutes before slicing.

← **GRAVY:** Meanwhile, skim fat from pan juices; bring juices to boil. In small bowl, whisk stock with flour; whisk into juices and simmer over medium heat, stirring occasionally, until thickened, about 5 minutes. Strain and serve with pork and vegetables.

PER SERVING OF 8: about 380 cal, 37 g pro, 12 g total fat (3 g sat. fat), 29 g carb, 2 fibre, 94 mg chol, 457 mg sodium. % RDI: 7% calcium, 16% iron, 171% vit A, 35% vit C, 9% folate.

PER 4 SERVINGS OF PORK ONLY: about 231 cal, 35 g pro, 8 g total fat (2 g sat. fat), 2 g carb, trace fibre, 94 mg chol, 294 mg sodium. % RDI: 4% calcium, 11% iron, 3% vit C, 4% folate.

TIP

CONVERT TO CONVECTION

Although you should consult the manufacturer's instructions, here are general rules when converting conventional oven recipes to convection.

← When roasting, reduce cooking time by about 25 per cent and cook at the same temperature as indicated in the original recipe.

← When baking, reduce oven temperature by 25°F (13°C), especially for less than 15 minutes baking time, and cook for the same length of time as indicated on the original recipe.

← Remember to write down the new cooking time or oven temperature on the conventional recipe for future reference.

GLAZED HAM WITH ORANGE CRANBERRY SAUCE

208 →

Because ham needs virtually no preparation before roasting and has a high ratio of servings to weight, it is a renowned centrepiece for a big gathering. We're pairing it with an orange-and-dried-cranberry sauce, which is a tangy new twist on a traditional raisin sauce.

Makes 24 to 30 servings

15 lb	fully cooked bone-in whole ham	**6.75 kg**
BROWN SUGAR GLAZE		
1 cup	packed brown sugar	**250 mL**
¼ cup	cider vinegar	**50 mL**
2 tbsp	Dijon mustard	**25 mL**
1 tbsp	grated orange rind	**15 mL**
ORANGE CRANBERRY SAUCE		
1 cup	dried cranberries	**250 mL**
1 tbsp	grated orange rind	**15 mL**
1 cup	each orange juice and water	**250 mL**
½ cup	packed brown sugar	**125 mL**
1 tbsp	cider vinegar	**15 mL**
1 tbsp	butter	**15 mL**
¼ tsp	cinnamon	**1 mL**
1 tbsp	cornstarch	**15 mL**

← Place ham, fat side up, on rack in roasting pan; pour 2 cups (500 mL) water into pan. Cover pan tightly with foil; roast in 325°F (160°C) oven for 3 hours.

← Remove ham from oven. If ham has skin, slide sharp knife under skin and lift off. Trim fat layer to ¼-inch (5 mm) thickness. Diagonally score fat side of ham to form diamond shapes.

← **BROWN SUGAR GLAZE:** In bowl, combine brown sugar, vinegar, mustard and orange rind; brush about one-third over ham. Roast, brushing twice more with mustard mixture, until crusty, caramel-colour and meat thermometer inserted in centre registers 140°F (60°C), about 1 hour. Transfer to cutting board and tent loosely with foil; let stand for 20 minutes.

← **ORANGE CRANBERRY SAUCE:** Meanwhile, in saucepan, bring cranberries, orange rind, orange juice, water, sugar, vinegar, butter and cinnamon to boil; reduce heat and simmer for 10 minutes. Whisk cornstarch with 2 tbsp (25 mL) water; whisk into saucepan and cook, stirring, until thickened, about 1 minute. *Make-ahead: Let cool; refrigerate in airtight container for up to 24 hours; rewarm to serve.*

← To carve, cut down to bone into ¼-inch (5 mm) thick slices. To cut off slices, hold knife parallel to bone and cut along bone. Turn remaining meaty portion up; repeat slicing. Serve with sauce.

PER EACH OF 30 SERVINGS: about 238 cal, 28 g pro, 7 g total fat (2 g sat. fat), 16 g carb, trace fibre, 63 mg chol, 1,509 mg sodium. % RDI: 2% calcium, 9% iron, 5% vit C, 3% folate.

VARIATION

GLAZED HAM WITH RED CURRANT GLAZE
Omit Brown Sugar Glaze. Combine ½ cup (125 mL) red currant jelly, 2 tbsp (25 mL) packed brown sugar and 4 tsp (20 mL) dry mustard. Continue with recipe.

FRESH PINEAPPLE SALSA

← 209

Try this zippy salsa instead of the cranberry sauce. There's enough for 15 servings, and it's easy to double.

Makes about 3½ cups (875 mL)

2 cups	chopped fresh pineapple (about half pineapple)	500 mL
1	mango, peeled and chopped	1
¼ cup	finely chopped red onion	50 mL
2 tbsp	orange juice	25 mL
1 tbsp	minced jalapeño pepper	15 mL
1 tbsp	finely chopped fresh mint	15 mL
1 tbsp	liquid honey	15 mL

← In bowl, combine pineapple, mango, onion, orange juice, jalapeño pepper, mint and honey. *Make-ahead: Cover and refrigerate for up to 24 hours.*

PER ¼ CUP (50 mL): about 27 cal, trace pro, trace total fat (0 g sat. fat), 7 g carb, 1 g fibre, 0 mg chol, 1 mg sodium. % RDI: 1% iron, 7% vit A, 17% vit C, 3% folate.

SPANISH CHICKEN WITH PEPPERS

Sweet red peppers, tomatoes, ham and a touch of paprika make a beautifully coloured and richly flavoured sauce for chicken. Serve with crusty bread or boiled or roasted potatoes.

Makes 6 servings

3 tbsp	all-purpose flour	50 mL
3 lb	chicken pieces, skinned	1.5 kg
2 tbsp	extra-virgin olive oil	25 mL
1	jar (370 mL) roasted whole sweet red peppers	1
⅔ cup	diced prosciutto or ham (about 3 oz/90 g)	150 mL
1	onion, sliced	1
4	cloves garlic, minced	4
1 tbsp	chopped fresh thyme (or 1 tsp/5 mL dried)	15 mL
2 tsp	paprika	10 mL
¼ tsp	each cayenne pepper and salt	1 mL
⅓ cup	dry white wine	75 mL
1	can (28 oz/796 mL) tomatoes, drained	1
⅓ cup	chopped fresh parsley	75 mL

← Pour flour into large plastic bag; add chicken, in batches, and shake to coat. Discard any remaining flour.

← In large nonstick skillet, heat half of the oil over medium-high heat; brown chicken, about 10 minutes. Transfer to plate. Drain fat from pan.

← Meanwhile, drain and thinly slice red peppers; set aside.

← Add remaining oil to pan. Fry red peppers, prosciutto, onion, garlic, thyme, paprika, cayenne and salt over medium heat, stirring occasionally, until onion is softened, about 5 minutes.

← Stir in wine and tomatoes, breaking up with spoon. Nestle chicken in sauce; bring to boil. Reduce heat, cover and simmer, occasionally spooning sauce over chicken, until juices run clear when chicken is pierced, 20 to 25 minutes. Sprinkle with parsley.

PER SERVING: about 286 cal, 34 g pro, 11 g total fat (2 g sat. fat), 13 g carb, 2 g fibre, 104 mg chol, 594 mg sodium. % RDI: 5% calcium, 18% iron, 27% vit A, 138% vit C, 14% folate.

CHICKEN WITH CREAMY PESTO SAUCE

212 →

Chicken breasts are a standby ingredient, but frankly, if it's flavour you like, they need help. Hence, here is a basil-mushroom sauce you can tart up with cream or keep lower in fat with evaporated milk.

Makes 4 servings

1 tbsp	vegetable oil	**15 mL**
4	boneless skinless chicken breasts	**4**
1	onion, chopped	**1**
2	cloves garlic, minced	**2**
3 cups	sliced mushrooms (8 oz/250 g)	**750 mL**
1 tsp	dried thyme	**5 mL**
½ tsp	salt	**2 mL**
¼ tsp	pepper	**1 mL**
½ cup	white wine or chicken stock	**125 mL**
1 tbsp	all-purpose flour	**15 mL**
1	can (384 mL) evaporated 2% milk	**1**
2 tbsp	basil pesto (or ⅓ cup/75 mL chopped fresh basil)	**25 mL**

← In large skillet or shallow Dutch oven, heat oil over medium-high heat; brown chicken, about 10 minutes. Transfer to plate.

← Add onion, garlic, mushrooms, thyme, salt and pepper; fry over medium heat, stirring occasionally, until no liquid from mushrooms remains, about 10 minutes.

← Add wine; cook, stirring, for 2 minutes. Whisk flour into evaporated milk; add to pan and cook, stirring, until thickened, about 5 minutes. Stir in pesto.

← Return chicken to pan, turning to coat; simmer until no longer pink inside, about 10 minutes.

PER SERVING: about 350 cal, 42 g pro, 11 g total fat (3 g sat. fat), 18 g carb, 1 g fibre, 93 mg chol, 570 mg sodium. % RDI: 31% calcium, 19% iron, 9% vit A, 20% vit C, 11% folate.

CHICKEN BACON BROCHETTES

Everything is better with bacon — even chunks of chicken. The bacon keeps the chicken moist and shares its delectable smokiness. Pair these brochettes with Asparagus Polonaise (recipe, opposite).

Makes 4 servings

1 lb	boneless skinless chicken breasts	**500 g**
2 tbsp	olive or vegetable oil	**25 mL**
2 tsp	each Worcestershire sauce and soy sauce	**10 mL**
½ tsp	wine vinegar	**2 mL**
2	cloves garlic, minced	**2**
¼ tsp	pepper	**1 mL**
12	large mushrooms	**12**
2 tsp	lemon juice	**10 mL**
¼ tsp	salt	**1 mL**
4	strips bacon, cut into thirds	**4**
4	green onions, cut into thirds	**4**

← Cut chicken into twelve 1½-inch (4 cm) cubes. In bowl, combine half of the oil, the Worcestershire sauce, soy sauce, vinegar, garlic and pepper; add chicken and marinate for 20 minutes.

← Meanwhile, in separate bowl, toss together mushrooms, remaining oil, lemon juice and salt; let stand for 20 minutes.

← Reserving marinade, wrap each chicken cube in bacon; thread onto 4 skewers alternately with mushrooms and green onions. *Make-ahead: Cover and refrigerate for up to 4 hours.*

← Place on greased grill over medium-high heat; close lid and grill for 5 minutes. Turn and brush with marinade; grill until chicken is no longer pink inside, 5 to 7 minutes.

PER SERVING: about 245 cal, 29 g pro, 12 g total fat (3 g sat. fat), 5 g carb, 1 g fibre, 72 mg chol, 509 mg sodium. % RDI: 2% calcium, 13% iron, 1% vit A, 7% vit C, 9% folate.

ASPARAGUS POLONAISE

← 215

Chopped egg yolk and egg white are the signature ingredients in any dish called "polonaise."

Makes 4 servings

1 lb	asparagus	500 g
¼ cup	butter	50 mL
2 tbsp	chopped fresh chives	25 mL
¼ tsp	each salt and pepper	1 mL
1	hard-cooked egg	1

← Snap off woody ends of asparagus. In wide skillet of boiling salted water, cover and cook asparagus until tender-crisp, 3 to 5 minutes. Drain and arrange on serving plate.

← Meanwhile, in skillet, melt butter with chives, salt and pepper. Separate egg white from yolk; chop white and add to pan. Pour over asparagus. Crumble yolk over top.

PER SERVING: about 140 cal, 4 g pro, 13 g total fat (8 g sat. fat), 4 g carb, 1 g fibre, 83 mg chol, 474 mg sodium. % RDI: 2% calcium, 6% iron, 18% vit A, 15% vit C, 56% folate.

LEMON AND OLIVE CHICKEN

Lemon and olives pique taste buds with lively flavours. Serve with potato wedges oven-roasted with olive oil.

Makes 6 servings

2 tbsp	extra-virgin olive oil	25 mL
3 lb	chicken pieces, skinned	1.5 kg
1	onion, chopped	1
3	cloves garlic, minced	3
2	bay leaves	2
1 tsp	each pepper, dried oregano and ground cumin and coriander	5 mL
½ tsp	salt	2 mL
¾ cup	chicken stock	175 mL
2 tbsp	lemon juice	25 mL
½ tsp	granulated sugar	2 mL
Half	lemon, thinly sliced	Half
3	plum tomatoes, cut into wedges	3
½ cup	pitted green or black olives	125 mL
¼ cup	chopped fresh parsley	50 mL

←217

← In large nonstick skillet, heat half of the oil over medium-high heat; brown chicken, about 10 minutes. Transfer to plate. Drain fat from pan.

← Add remaining oil to pan. Fry onion, garlic, bay leaves, pepper, oregano, cumin, coriander and salt over medium heat, stirring occasionally, until onion is softened, about 5 minutes.

← Return chicken to pan. Add stock, lemon juice and sugar; arrange lemon slices over chicken. Reduce heat, cover and simmer, occasionally spooning sauce over chicken, for 15 minutes.

← Add tomatoes and olives; cook, uncovered, until juices run clear when chicken is pierced, 5 to 10 minutes. Discard bay leaves. Sprinkle with parsley.

PER SERVING: about 246 cal, 31 g pro, 11 g total fat (2 g sat. fat), 6 g carb, 1 g fibre, 96 mg chol, 684 mg sodium. % RDI: 4% calcium, 15% iron, 7% vit A, 35% vit C, 7% folate.

SWEET-AND-SOUR BAKED CHICKEN WITH CARROTS

Here's the recipe to try with those thrifty family-size packs of chicken legs.

Makes 6 servings

2	onions	2
4	carrots	4
2	sweet green peppers	2
6	chicken legs	6
¼ cup	all-purpose flour	50 mL
½ tsp	each salt and pepper	2 mL
2 tbsp	vegetable oil	25 mL
½ cup	orange juice	125 mL
¼ cup	liquid honey	50 mL
¼ cup	soy sauce	50 mL
¼ cup	tomato paste	50 mL
1 tbsp	cornstarch	15 mL
3	cloves garlic, minced	3

←219

← Cut each onion into 6 wedges. Cut carrots into ½-inch (1 cm) chunks. Seed, core and cut green peppers into 1-inch (2.5 cm) pieces. Scatter vegetables in large roasting pan; cover and roast in 400°F (200°C) oven until slightly tender, about 10 minutes.

← Meanwhile, grasp skin at end of each chicken thigh with paper towel; pull to bony end of drumstick and cut off skin at bony end with sharp knife.

← In large shallow dish, combine flour, salt and pepper; press chicken into mixture to coat all over. In large nonstick skillet, heat 1 tbsp (15 mL) of the oil over medium-high heat; brown chicken, in batches and adding remaining oil as necessary, about 8 minutes. Arrange on vegetables.

← In measuring cup, whisk together orange juice, honey, soy sauce, tomato paste, cornstarch and garlic; pour over chicken and vegetables. Cover and roast for 20 minutes; uncover and roast, basting occasionally, until chicken is golden and juices run clear when legs are pierced, about 20 minutes.

PER SERVING: about 386 cal, 35 g pro, 13 g total fat (3 g sat. fat), 33 g carb, 3 g fibre, 130 mg chol, 1,061 mg sodium. % RDI: 5% calcium, 23% iron, 128% vit A, 77% vit C, 19% folate.

POTATO-TOPPED CHICKEN POT PIES

220 →

These make-ahead tasty meals, with their golden potato topping, are comfort food to the max.

Makes 4 servings

1 lb	boneless skinless chicken breasts or thighs	500 g
2 cups	chicken stock	500 mL
2 cups	button mushrooms, quartered	500 mL
1	onion, chopped	1
2	carrots, chopped	2
2	cloves garlic, minced	2
2	bay leaves	2
¼ tsp	each salt and pepper	1 mL
Pinch	nutmeg	Pinch
1 cup	frozen peas	250 mL
1 tsp	Dijon mustard	5 mL
½ tsp	lemon juice	2 mL
½ cup	all-purpose flour	125 mL
TOPPING		
6	Yukon Gold potatoes (1½ lb/750 g)	6
½ cup	each milk and cream cheese	125 mL
2 tbsp	butter	25 mL
½ tsp	each salt and pepper	2 mL

← TOPPING: Peel potatoes and cut into ½-inch (1 cm) chunks. In large saucepan of boiling salted water, cover and cook potatoes until tender, about 15 minutes; drain and return to pot. Add milk, cheese, butter, salt and pepper; mash until smooth. Set aside.

← Meanwhile, cut chicken into ½-inch (1 cm) chunks. In separate large saucepan, bring stock to boil. Add chicken, mushrooms, onion, carrots, garlic, bay leaves, salt, pepper and nutmeg; reduce heat, cover and simmer until chicken is no longer pink inside, about 6 minutes. Stir in peas, mustard and lemon juice.

← In small bowl, whisk flour with ⅓ cup (75 mL) cold water; whisk into chicken mixture and bring to boil. Reduce heat and cook, stirring often, until sauce is thick enough to coat back of spoon, about 5 minutes.

← Ladle into four 2-cup (500 mL) ovenproof or foil dishes or 10-cup (2.5 L) casserole dish. Spoon or pipe potato mixture over top; cover with foil. *Make-ahead: Let cool for 30 minutes; refrigerate until cold. Cover with foil and overwrap with heavy-duty foil; freeze for up to 1 month. Thaw in refrigerator; remove heavy-duty foil.*

← Bake on rimmed baking sheet in 400°F (200°C) oven until knife inserted in centre for 5 seconds feels hot when touched, 20 to 25 minutes. Uncover and broil until golden, about 3 minutes.

PER SERVING: about 582 cal, 40 g pro, 20 g total fat (11 g sat. fat), 62 g carb, 7 g fibre, 118 mg chol, 1,122 mg sodium. % RDI: 11% calcium, 29% iron, 112% vit A, 35% vit C, 37% folate.

CHUNKY CHICKEN IN DIJON CHEDDAR SAUCE

This dish takes about 25 minutes to make — just the time it takes to cook a pot of spinach noodles or potatoes to mash and serve alongside.

Makes 4 servings

1 lb	boneless skinless chicken thighs or breasts	500 g
1 tbsp	vegetable oil	15 mL
1	onion, finely chopped	1
2	cloves garlic, minced	2
¼ tsp	each salt, pepper and dried thyme	1 mL
3 tbsp	all-purpose flour	50 mL
1½ cups	milk	375 mL
2 tbsp	Dijon mustard	25 mL
Dash	hot pepper sauce	Dash
1 cup	shredded extra-old Cheddar cheese	250 mL
¼ cup	finely diced sweet red or green pepper	50 mL
¼ cup	minced fresh parsley	50 mL

↩ 223

↩ Cut chicken into bite-size pieces. In large skillet, heat oil over medium-high heat; brown chicken, in batches. Transfer to plate. Drain fat from pan.

↩ Add onion, garlic, salt, pepper and thyme to pan; fry over medium heat, stirring often, until softened, about 5 minutes.

↩ Sprinkle with flour; cook, stirring, for 1 minute. Whisk in milk; cook, whisking, until thickened, about 5 minutes. Stir in mustard and hot pepper sauce.

↩ Return chicken and any juices to pan; cover and simmer until juices run clear when chicken is pierced, about 10 minutes.

↩ Add cheese and half each of the red pepper and parsley; stir until cheese is melted. Sprinkle each serving with remaining red pepper and parsley.

PER SERVING: about 379 cal, 33 g pro, 21 g total fat (9 g sat. fat), 13 g carb, 1 g fibre, 131 mg chol, 566 mg sodium. % RDI: 32% calcium, 16% iron, 20% vit A 43% vit C, 15% folate.

CHICKEN, SNOW PEAS AND CASHEW STIR-FRY

224 →

Stir-fries are great year-round meals — quick, healthy and popular with kids. Serve with quick-cooking Asian noodles, such as chow mein or rice vermicelli.

Makes 4 servings

3 tbsp	soy sauce	50 mL
4 tsp	cornstarch	20 mL
1 tbsp	granulated sugar	15 mL
1 tbsp	sherry or chicken stock	15 mL
1 tsp	sesame oil	5 mL
Dash	hot pepper sauce	Dash
1 lb	boneless skinless chicken thighs or breasts	500 g
1 cup	snow peas (4 oz/125 g)	250 mL
1	sweet red pepper	1
1 tbsp	vegetable oil	15 mL
⅓ cup	roasted cashews	75 mL
1	clove garlic, sliced	1
1	piece (2 inches/5 cm) gingerroot, sliced	1

← In small bowl, whisk together soy sauce, cornstarch, sugar, sherry, sesame oil and hot pepper sauce; set aside. Cut chicken into bite-size pieces; set aside.

← Remove strings from snow peas; cut diagonally in half. Seed, core and cut red pepper into bite-size chunks. Set aside.

← In wok or large skillet, heat vegetable oil over high heat; stir-fry chicken, in batches, until browned, about 3 minutes. Transfer to plate.

← Add snow peas, red pepper, cashews, garlic and ginger to wok; cover and steam until red pepper is tender-crisp, about 2 minutes.

← Return chicken and any accumulated juices to pan; toss to combine. Stir in soy sauce mixture; simmer until glossy, about 1 minute.

PER SERVING: about 303 cal, 25 g pro, 16 g total fat (3 g sat. fat), 15 g carb, 2 g fibre, 94 mg chol, 876 mg sodium. % RDI: 3% calcium, 18% iron, 13% vit A, 102% vit C, 12% folate.

GARLIC LEMON CHICKEN

Sunny, lemony and redolent of garlic, this dish is a crowd-pleaser. If you make it ahead, you can use all chicken thighs instead of chicken pieces — they stay extra moist when reheated.

Makes 8 servings

3½ lb	chicken pieces	1.75 kg
1 tbsp	vegetable oil	15 mL
1	lemon, cut into wedges	1
¼ cup	lemon juice	50 mL
20	cloves garlic	20
2 tbsp	chopped fresh oregano (or 1 tsp/5 mL dried)	25 mL
½ tsp	each salt and pepper	2 mL
1 tbsp	chopped fresh parsley	15 mL

← 227

← Cut any large chicken pieces in half. In large nonstick skillet, heat oil over medium-high heat; brown chicken, in batches, about 5 minutes. Drain off fat.

← Arrange chicken and lemon wedges in 13- x 9-inch (3 L) glass baking dish. Sprinkle with lemon juice, garlic, oregano, salt and pepper.

← Bake in 425°F (220°C) oven, turning and basting twice, until breasts are no longer pink inside and juices run clear when thighs are pierced, about 30 minutes. *Make-ahead: Let cool for 30 minutes. Refrigerate until cold; cover with foil and refrigerate for up to 24 hours. Reheat, covered, in 375°F (190°C) oven, basting once, for 15 minutes.* Sprinkle with parsley.

PER SERVING: about 237 cal, 24 g pro, 14 g total fat (3 g sat. fat), 3 g carb, trace fibre, 77 mg chol, 217 mg sodium. % RDI: 3% calcium, 9% iron, 4% vit A, 8% vit C, 3% folate.

ROAST TURKEY WITH HERBED STUFFING

228 →

For important holidays, you need the impressive bird — turkey! This recipe is easy to follow, even for a turkey-roasting novice, and is guaranteed to succeed.

Makes 8 to 10 servings

15 lb	turkey	6.75 kg
¼ cup	butter, softened	50 mL
½ tsp	each dried sage and thyme	2 mL
1 tsp	each salt and pepper	5 mL

HERBED STUFFING

¾ cup	butter	175 mL
2½ cups	chopped onions	625 mL
1 cup	each chopped celery and fennel (or 2 cups/500 mL celery)	250 mL
4 tsp	dried sage	20 mL
1 tsp	each salt, dried savory, marjoram and pepper	5 mL
½ tsp	dried thyme	2 mL
14 cups	cubed white bread	3.5 L
1 cup	chopped fresh parsley	250 mL

STOCK

4½ cups	chicken stock	1.125 L
1½ cups	dry white wine or water (approx)	375 mL
1	onion, chopped	1
½ cup	each sliced carrot and celery	125 mL

GRAVY

¼ cup	all-purpose flour	50 mL
2 tbsp	butter	25 mL
½ tsp	each salt and pepper	2 mL

← **HERBED STUFFING:** In large skillet, melt butter over medium heat; fry onions, celery, fennel, sage, salt, savory, marjoram, pepper and thyme, stirring often, until vegetables are tender, 10 to 15 minutes. Transfer to large bowl. Add bread and parsley; toss to combine. Set aside. *Make-ahead: Let cool; refrigerate in airtight container for up to 24 hours.*

← Remove giblets and neck from turkey; place in large saucepan and set aside.

← Pat turkey dry inside and out. Loosely fill neck cavity with stuffing; fold neck skin over stuffing and skewer to back. Lift wings and twist under back. Stuff body cavity. Tuck legs under band of skin or tie together with string.

← Immediately place turkey, breast side up, on rack in roasting pan. In small bowl, mix together butter, sage and thyme; rub over turkey. Sprinkle with salt and pepper. Tent with foil, dull side out, leaving sides open.

← Roast in 325°F (160°C) oven, basting every 30 minutes, for 4 hours. Remove foil; roast until meat thermometer inserted in thigh registers 185°F (85°C) and stuffing 165°F (74°C), about 1 hour longer. Transfer to cutting board; tent with foil and let stand for 20 minutes.

← **STOCK:** Meanwhile, to saucepan with turkey parts, add stock, wine, onion, carrot and celery; bring to boil. Reduce heat to low and skim off fat; simmer for 3 hours. Strain into measuring cup, adding enough wine to make 3 cups (750 mL). Set aside.

← 229

← **GRAVY:** Skim off fat in roasting pan. Stir flour into pan; cook over medium heat, stirring, for 1 minute. Whisk in stock and bring to boil, stirring to scrape up brown bits; reduce heat and simmer for 5 minutes. Whisk in butter, salt and pepper. Strain if desired.

← With carving knife and fork, cut legs from turkey, twisting loose if necessary. Cut thigh from drumstick at joint; carve dark meat from each piece. Cut off wings. With tip of knife toward body cavity, carve breast thinly, gradually angling knife to slice thick part of breast.

PER EACH OF 10 SERVINGS: about 693 cal, 67 g pro, 33 g total fat (16 g sat. fat), 28 g carb, 3 g fibre, 219 mg chol, 1,500 mg sodium. % RDI: 13% calcium, 46% iron, 22% vit A, 17% vit C, 31% folate.

TURKEY ENCHILADAS

230 → As sure as there's turkey, there will be leftovers. Here's a fabulous way to enjoy big bird encores.

Makes 8 servings

2 tsp	vegetable oil	10 mL
3	cloves garlic, minced	3
1	small onion, chopped	1
4	large mushrooms, finely chopped	4
4 cups	cubed cooked turkey or chicken	1 L
1	can (19 oz/540 mL) black beans, drained and rinsed	1
1½ cups	shredded Cheddar cheese	375 mL
1½ cups	shredded jalapeño Monterey Jack cheese	375 mL
1 cup	sour cream	250 mL
8	large flour tortillas	8
3 cups	salsa	750 mL

← In skillet, heat oil over medium heat; fry garlic, onion and mushrooms, stirring occasionally, until no liquid from mushrooms remains, about 6 minutes. Remove from heat.

← Stir in turkey, beans, 1 cup (250 mL) each of the Cheddar and Monterey Jack cheeses and sour cream.

← Place 1 tortilla on work surface; spoon about ¾ cup (175 mL) of the filling along centre. Fold bottom edge over filling; fold in sides and roll up. Place, seam side down, in greased 13- x 9-inch (3 L) glass baking dish. Repeat with remaining tortillas and filling. Top with salsa; cover with foil.

← Bake in 375°F (190°C) oven until knife inserted in centre comes out hot, about 35 minutes. Uncover; sprinkle with remaining cheeses. Bake until cheese melts, about 10 minutes.

PER SERVING: about 611 cal, 42 g pro, 27 g total fat (13 g sat. fat), 51 g carb, 7 g fibre, 106 mg chol, 941 mg sodium. % RDI: 40% calcium, 38% iron, 21% vit A, 33% vit C, 47% folate.

TIP

Instead of jalapeño Monterey Jack cheese, you can use regular Monterey Jack and ¼ cup (50 mL) finely chopped pickled or fresh jalapeños.

PARMESAN CHICKEN STRIPS WITH TOMATO DIPPING SAUCE

Crushed melba toast is the key to really crunchy chicken strips or fingers.

Makes 4 servings

4	boneless skinless chicken breasts	4
16	melba toasts	16
2 tbsp	grated Parmesan cheese	25 mL
1 tsp	dried oregano	5 mL
¼ tsp	each salt and pepper	1 mL
1	egg	1
1 tbsp	vegetable oil	15 mL

TOMATO DIPPING SAUCE

1	can (14 oz/398 mL) tomatoes	1
¼ cup	tomato paste	50 mL
2	green onions, chopped	2
1 tsp	dried basil	5 mL
¼ tsp	each salt and pepper	1 mL

← **TOMATO DIPPING SAUCE:** In saucepan and using potato masher, crush tomatoes into small pieces. Add tomato paste, green onions, basil, salt and pepper; bring to boil over high heat. Reduce heat to medium-low; simmer, stirring occasionally, until thick enough to mound on spoon, about 20 minutes. *Make-ahead: Let cool for 30 minutes. Refrigerate, uncovered, in airtight container until cold; cover and refrigerate for up to 2 days.*

← Meanwhile cut chicken lengthwise into 1-inch (2.5 cm) thick strips. In food processor or plastic bag and using rolling pin, crush melba toasts into crumbs; transfer to shallow dish. Add Parmesan cheese, oregano, salt and pepper; toss to combine. In another shallow dish, whisk egg. Dip each chicken strip into egg, letting excess drip off; dip into crumb mixture, turning and pressing to coat.

← In large nonstick skillet, heat oil over medium-high heat; fry chicken, in batches and turning halfway through, until golden and no longer pink inside, about 10 minutes. Serve with sauce.

←233

PER SERVING: about 326 cal, 37 g pro, 9 g total fat (2 g sat. fat), 24 g carb, 3 g fibre, 126 mg chol, 761 mg sodium. % RDI: 11% calcium, 20% iron, 13% vit A, 38% vit C, 21% folate.

CHAPTER 7

FISH, EG
AND
VEGETA

GS

RIAN

← 237

CATFISH FINGERS WITH CAJUN MAYONNAISE

Farmed catfish is mild and cooks in a flash. Perfect for busy-night meals.

Makes 4 servings

1 lb	catfish fillets	500 g
¼ tsp	each salt and pepper	1 mL
½ cup	cornmeal	125 mL
2 tsp	vegetable oil	10 mL
CAJUN MAYONNAISE		
⅓ cup	light mayonnaise	75 mL
1	green onion, thinly sliced	1
1½ tsp	lemon juice	7 mL
1 tsp	Cajun seasoning	5 mL

← Cut catfish crosswise into 1-inch (2.5 cm) wide strips; sprinkle with salt and pepper. Sprinkle cornmeal in shallow dish; press fish into cornmeal, turning to coat.

← Brush oil over rimmed baking sheet; heat in 450°F (230°C) oven for 5 minutes. Arrange catfish on prepared sheet; bake, turning once, until golden and fish flakes easily when tested, about 10 minutes.

← **CAJUN MAYONNAISE:** Meanwhile, in bowl, stir together mayonnaise, onion, lemon juice and Cajun seasoning. Serve with fish.

PER SERVING: about 256 cal, 22 g pro, 11 g total fat (2 g sat. fat), 16 g carb, 1 g fibre, 59 mg chol, 412 mg sodium. % RDI: 1% calcium, 4% iron, 14% vit A, 3% vit C, 6% folate.

BROCCOLI AND CAULIFLOWER

Pop this into the oven while the catfish is baking.

Makes 4 servings

2 cups	each broccoli and cauliflower florets	500 mL
2	cloves garlic, minced	2
¼ cup	chicken stock	50 mL
1 tbsp	butter	15 mL

← In 6-cup (1.5 L) casserole, combine broccoli and cauliflower. Sprinkle with garlic and chicken stock; dot with butter. Cover and bake in 450°F (230°C) oven until tender-crisp, 8 to 10 minutes.

PER SERVING: about 48 cal, 2 g pro, 3 g total fat (2 g sat. fat), 4 g carb, 2 g fibre, 9 mg chol, 92 mg sodium. % RDI: 2% calcium, 3% iron, 6% vit A, 65% vit C 15% folate.

GARLIC GRATIN FISH

Fish is the ultimate quick-dinner solution for time-crunched cooks. Cod, haddock, trout, tilapia or halibut fillets that are about 1 inch (2.5 cm) thick are ideal.

242 →

Makes 4 servings

1 cup	fresh bread crumbs	250 mL
2 tbsp	butter, melted	25 mL
2 tsp	chopped fresh oregano (or ½ tsp/2 mL dried)	10 mL
1 tsp	grated lemon rind	5 mL
2	cloves garlic, minced	2
¼ tsp	each salt and pepper	1 mL
1 lb	fish fillets	500 g
1 tbsp	Dijon mustard	15 mL
	Lemon wedges	

← In small bowl, toss together bread crumbs, butter, oregano, lemon rind and garlic. Sprinkle salt and pepper all over fillets; place on greased foil-lined rimmed baking sheet. Brush with mustard; evenly spoon crumb mixture over top.

← Bake in 450°F (230°C) oven until topping is golden and crisp and fish flakes easily when tested, 10 to 15 minutes. Serve with lemon wedges to squeeze over top.

PER SERVING: about 179 cal, 21 g pro, 7 g total fat (4 g sat. fat), 6 g carb, trace fibre, 64 mg chol, 371 mg sodium. % RDI: 4% calcium, 6% iron, 7% vit A, 3% vit C, 8% folate.

SALMON FILLET ON SPINACH SALAD

Serving a hot item, such as these seasoned salmon fillets, over a salad is a restaurant-style presentation. Why not borrow it for a quick dinner for family or company?

Makes 4 servings

4	salmon fillets (each 6 oz/175 g)	4
½ tsp	pepper	2 mL
¼ tsp	salt	1 mL
3 tbsp	extra-virgin olive oil	50 mL
Half	small red onion, thinly sliced	Half
2 tbsp	grainy mustard	25 mL
2 tbsp	wine vinegar	25 mL
1	pkg (10 oz/284 g) fresh spinach	1

↞ Season salmon with half each of the pepper and salt. In large skillet, heat 1 tbsp (15 mL) of the oil over medium-high heat. Add salmon, skin side down; cover and fry, turning once, until fish flakes easily when tested, about 12 minutes. Transfer to plate and keep warm. Drain fat from pan.

↞ In same pan, heat remaining oil over low heat; fry onion until softened, about 2 minutes. Whisk in mustard, vinegar and remaining salt and pepper.

↞ Place spinach in bowl; pour vinaigrette over top and toss to coat. Divide among 4 plates; nestle salmon in centre of each.

PER SERVING: about 411 cal, 34 g pro, 28 g total fat (5 g sat. fat), 7 g carb, 2 g fibre, 91 mg chol, 392 mg sodium. % RDI: 10% calcium, 21% iron, 50% vit A, 43% vit C, 81% folate.

BOILED DILL POTATOES

Instead of eight small new potatoes, you can use four potatoes, halved.

Makes 4 servings

8	small new potatoes	8
1 tbsp	butter or extra-virgin olive oil	15 mL
¼ tsp	each dried dillweed, salt and pepper	1 mL

↞ In saucepan of boiling salted water, cover and boil potatoes until tender, about 15 minutes. Drain and return to pan. Add butter, dillweed, salt and pepper; toss to coat.

PER SERVING: about 76 cal, 1 g pro, 3 g total fat (2 g sat. fat), 12 g carb, 1 g fibre, 9 mg chol, 312 mg sodium. % RDI: 1% calcium, 4% iron, 3% vit A, 12% vit C, 3% folate.

TUNA PATTIES

These crispy patties may not be crab cakes, but they sure are good and disappear like magic. We like them with salsa or seafood sauce and a salad.

Makes 4 servings

20	soda crackers	20
3	cans (each 170 g) water-packed tuna, drained	3
1	onion, chopped	1
2	cloves garlic, minced	2
1	egg, beaten	1
⅓ cup	light mayonnaise	75 mL
2 tbsp	chopped fresh coriander or parsley	25 mL
2 tbsp	dill pickle relish	25 mL
1 tbsp	lemon juice	15 mL
¼ tsp	each salt and pepper	1 mL
1 tbsp	vegetable oil	15 mL

←247

← In food processor or plastic bag and using rolling pin, coarsely crush crackers; place in bowl. Add tuna, onion, garlic, egg, mayonnaise, coriander, relish, lemon juice, salt and pepper. Using wet hands, shape into eight ½-inch (1 cm) thick patties. *Make-ahead: Place on waxed paper-lined tray; cover and refrigerate for up to 24 hours.*

← In large nonstick skillet, heat oil over medium-high heat; fry patties, turning once, until golden and crisp, about 8 minutes.

PER SERVING: about 308 cal, 29 g pro, 13 g total fat (2 g sat. fat), 16 g carb, 1 g fibre, 83 mg chol, 904 mg sodium. % RDI: 4% calcium, 19% iron, 4% vit A, 3% vit C, 15% folate.

SPICED-BAKED COD

There's a real nip to the spice mixture coating the fish. Reduce the cayenne and black pepper for timid tastes.

Makes 4 servings

1 tsp	salt	5 mL
½ tsp	each dried oregano, cayenne pepper, paprika, black pepper, crushed fennel seeds and thyme	2 mL
4	cod fillets (2 lb/1 kg), at least 1 inch (2.5 cm) thick	4
2 tbsp	extra-virgin olive oil	25 mL

← In small bowl, combine salt, oregano, cayenne, paprika, black pepper, fennel seeds and thyme. Sprinkle over 1 side of fillets and rub in with fingers.
← In large ovenproof skillet, heat oil over medium-high heat; fry fillets, spice side down, until browned, about 2 minutes. With large spatula, turn fillets. Bake in 400°F (200°C) oven or continue frying until fish flakes easily when tested, about 5 minutes.

PER SERVING: about 249 cal, 41 g pro, 8 g total fat (1 g sat. fat), 1 g carb, trace fibre, 97 mg chol, 712 mg sodium. % RDI: 3% calcium, 9% iron, 5% vit A, 3% vit C, 9% folate.

LIMA BEAN CORN MEDLEY

Your freezer is your friend when it comes to quick side dishes.

Makes 4 servings

2 tbsp	butter	25 mL
1	onion chopped	1
¼ tsp	each salt, pepper and dried thyme	1 mL
1 cup	frozen lima beans	250 mL
1 cup	frozen corn kernels	250 mL
1	can (19 oz/540 mL) diced tomatoes, drained	1

← In saucepan, melt butter over medium heat; fry onion, salt, pepper and thyme, stirring occasionally, until softened, about 3 minutes. Add lima beans, corn and tomatoes; cook, stirring, until heated through, about 5 minutes.

PER SERVING: about 159 cal, 5 g pro, 6 g total fat (4 g sat. fat), 23 g carb, 4 g fibre, 18 mg chol, 365 mg sodium. % RDI: 4% calcium, 13% iron, 12% vit A, 23% vit C, 14% folate.

SALMON WITH LENTIL PILAF

250 →

Lentils, like beans, add healthy fibre to your diet. And, since they don't require any soaking, lentils are the ultimate convenience legume.

Makes 4 servings

4	salmon fillets (each 6 oz/175 g)	4
2 tbsp	vegetable oil	25 mL
¼ tsp	each salt and pepper	1 mL
1 tbsp	chopped fresh mint or parsley	15 mL
LENTIL PILAF		
1 tbsp	vegetable oil	15 mL
1	onion, chopped	1
1	stalk celery, chopped	1
2	cloves garlic, minced	2
1	sweet red pepper, diced	1
1 tsp	ground cumin	5 mL
¼ tsp	salt	1 mL
1 cup	brown or green lentils	250 mL
2 cups	chicken stock	500 mL
2 tbsp	chopped fresh mint or parsley	25 mL

← LENTIL PILAF: In saucepan, heat oil over medium heat; fry onion, celery, garlic, red pepper, cumin and salt, stirring occasionally, until onion is softened, about 5 minutes.

← Add lentils; stir to coat. Add stock; bring to boil. Reduce heat, cover and simmer until lentils are tender and some liquid remains, about 40 minutes. Stir in mint.

← Meanwhile, place salmon on parchment paper–lined or greased rimmed baking sheet. Brush with oil; sprinkle with salt and pepper. Roast in 425°F (220°C) oven until fish flakes easily when tested, about 12 minutes. Sprinkle with mint.

← Arrange lentil pilaf on warmed plates; top with salmon.

PER SERVING: about 570 cal, 45 g pro, 28 g total fat (4 g sat. fat), 34 g carb, 7 g fibre, 84 mg chol, 770 mg sodium. % RDI: 7% calcium, 44% iron, 14% vit A, 97% vit C, 142% folate.

RICE AND GREENS WITH SHRIMP

Here's a tip that makes shredding leafy vegetables and herbs easier. Roll the leaves into a cigar shape, then cut them crosswise. Ta-dah — chefs call this chiffonade!

Makes 4 servings

1 tbsp	extra-virgin olive oil	**15 mL**
1	onion, chopped	**1**
4	cloves garlic, minced	**4**
¼ tsp	each salt and pepper	**1 mL**
1⅓ cups	long-grain rice	**325 mL**
2⅔ cups	chicken stock	**650 mL**
1 tsp	grated lemon rind	**5 mL**
1 lb	large shrimp, peeled and deveined	**500 g**
3 cups	packed Swiss chard or spinach, coarsely shredded	**750 mL**
1 tbsp	chopped fresh dill	**15 mL**
1 tbsp	lemon juice	**15 mL**
	Lemon wedges	

←253

← In large saucepan, heat oil over medium heat; fry onion, garlic, salt and pepper, stirring occasionally, until softened, about 5 minutes. Stir in rice.

← Add stock and lemon rind; bring to boil. Reduce heat, cover and simmer until liquid is almost absorbed, about 15 minutes.

← With fork, gently stir shrimp, Swiss chard, dill and lemon juice into rice mixture; cover and cook until shrimp are pink and greens are wilted, about 5 minutes. Serve with lemon wedges.

PER SERVING: about 394 cal, 27 g pro, 6 g total fat (1 g sat. fat), 55 g carb, 2 g fibre, 129 mg chol, 821 mg sodium. % RDI: 10% calcium, 28% iron, 37% vit A, 15% vit C, 35% folate.

VARIATION

VEGETARIAN RICE AND GREENS

Omit shrimp. Replace chicken stock with vegetable stock. Serve sprinkled with ½ cup (125 mL) crumbled feta cheese, if desired.

SPINACH AND SOLE WITH FINES HERBES

A light fish dinner with fresh greens is a welcome reprieve for family and entertaining dinners. Sweet potatoes or wild rice are fine sides.

Makes 4 servings

¼ cup	all-purpose flour	50 mL
¼ tsp	each salt and pepper	1 mL
4	sole fillets (total 1½ lb/750 g)	4
2 tbsp	extra-virgin olive oil	25 mL
1	pkg (10 oz/284 g) fresh spinach, coarsely chopped	1
1 tbsp	fines herbes	15 mL
Half	lemon, quartered	Half

◁255

◀ In shallow dish, combine flour, salt and pepper. One at a time, dip fillets into flour mixture, turning to coat; shake off excess.

◀ In large nonstick skillet, heat 1 tbsp (15 mL) of the oil over medium-high heat; fry fish, in 2 batches and adding remaining oil, until crispy and golden, 2 to 3 minutes per side. Transfer to plate; keep warm.

◀ Add spinach, fines herbes and 2 tbsp (25 mL) water to pan. Reduce heat to medium; cover and steam, stirring once, until spinach is tender, about 3 minutes. Serve with fish and lemon wedges.

PER SERVING: about 262 cal, 35 g pro, 9 g total fat (1 g sat. fat), 9 g carb, 2 g fibre, 82 mg chol, 329 mg sodium. % RDI: 12% calcium, 26% iron, 58% vit A, 17% vit C, 55% folate.

TIP

You can make your own fines herbes, which are equal parts of chopped dried chives, parsley and tarragon.

15-MINUTE ROASTED TROUT

If you have a large microwave oven, you can cook the onions right in the baking dish and save on cleanup.

Makes 4 servings

2 cups	thinly sliced onions	500 mL
2	cloves garlic, minced	2
1 tbsp	extra-virgin olive oil	15 mL
½ tsp	each salt and pepper	2 mL
4	trout or salmon fillets (each 6 oz/175 g)	4
GREMOLADA		
¼ cup	finely chopped fresh parsley	50 mL
2 tsp	finely grated lemon rind	10 mL
1	clove garlic, minced	1

← In microwaveable bowl, combine onions, garlic, oil, salt and pepper; cover and microwave at high, stirring twice, until softened, about 5 minutes.

← **GREMOLADA:** Meanwhile, in small bowl, combine parsley, lemon rind and garlic; set aside.

← Spread onion mixture in 13- x 9-inch (3 L) glass baking dish. Arrange fish over top; sprinkle with Gremolada.

← Roast fish in bottom third of 425°F (220°C) oven until fish flakes easily when tested, about 10 minutes.

PER SERVING: about 281 cal, 33 g pro, 13 g total fat (3 g sat. fat), 6 g carb, 1 g fibre, 90 mg chol, 347 mg sodium. % RDI: 12% calcium, 6% iron, 13% vit A, 22% vit C, 20% folate.

OVEN-CRISP EGG FOO YONG

To speed things up and free up the stove, cover and microwave the rice, 1¾ cups (425 mL) water and salt at high for 8 minutes, then at medium for 6 minutes.

Makes 4 servings

1 cup	long-grain rice	250 mL
½ tsp	salt	2 mL
½ cup	plum sauce	125 mL
2 tbsp	soy sauce	25 mL
Dash	sesame oil (optional)	Dash
1 tsp	vegetable oil	5 mL
8	eggs, lightly beaten	8
¼ cup	sliced green onions	50 mL
¼ cup	chopped sweet red pepper	50 mL
1 cup	bean sprouts	250 mL

←259

← In saucepan, bring 2 cups (500 mL) water to boil; stir in rice and salt. Cover and reduce heat to low; simmer until tender and water is absorbed, about 20 minutes.

← Meanwhile, in bowl, whisk together plum sauce, soy sauce, and sesame oil (if using); set aside.

← Meanwhile, in large nonstick ovenproof skillet, heat oil over medium heat. Pour in eggs; sprinkle with onions and red pepper. Cook, without stirring, for 4 minutes. Broil until set and golden, about 2 minutes. Sprinkle with bean sprouts. Serve with rice and sauce.

PER SERVING: about 392 cal, 17 g pro, 12 g total fat (3 g sat. fat), 52 g carb, 1 g fibre, 429 mg chol, 956 mg sodium. % RDI: 7% calcium, 16% iron, 22% vit A, 23% vit C, 27% folate.

TIP

Instead of bean sprouts, you can use chopped fresh coriander, parsley or chervil.

PIZZA OMELETTE

260 → Here's a dish that kids can help make. They delight in breaking the eggs, and if any shell gets into the eggs, the children can learn how to use a bigger piece of shell to fish it out.

Makes 4 servings

1 tbsp	vegetable oil	**15 mL**
1	onion, chopped	**1**
Half	sweet green pepper, diced	**Half**
1 cup	sliced mushrooms	**250 mL**
¾ cup	sliced pepperoni	**175 mL**
1 tsp	dried oregano	**5 mL**
6	eggs	**6**
¼ tsp	pepper	**1 mL**
1 cup	pasta sauce	**250 mL**
½ cup	shredded provolone or mozzarella cheese	**125 mL**

← In 9- or 10-inch (23 or 25 cm) nonstick ovenproof skillet, heat oil over medium heat; fry onion, green pepper, mushrooms, pepperoni and oregano, stirring occasionally, until onion is softened, about 5 minutes.

← In bowl, whisk eggs with pepper; pour over vegetable mixture and stir to combine. Bake in 400°F (200°C) oven until top is firm, about 8 minutes.

← Spread pasta sauce over top; sprinkle with cheese. Bake until cheese is bubbly, about 4 minutes.

PER SERVING: about 373 cal, 20 g pro, 28 g total fat (9 g sat. fat), 11 g carb, 2 g fibre, 310 mg chol, 1,009 mg sodium. % RDI: 15% calcium, 16% iron, 19% vit A, 28% vit C, 24% folate.

BROCCOLI CHEDDAR STRATA

Prepare this when you need a make-ahead casserole for dinner, lunch and even weekend brunch.

Makes 6 to 8 servings

1	loaf (1 lb/500 g) day-old egg bread or home-style white bread	1
6	eggs	6
2 cups	milk	500 mL
1 tbsp	Dijon mustard	15 mL
½ tsp	each salt and pepper	2 mL
2 cups	frozen or cooked fresh broccoli florets	500 mL
1½ cups	shredded old Cheddar cheese	375 mL
4	green onions, sliced	4

← Cut bread into ¾-inch (2 cm) cubes to make 12 cups (3 L); set aside.

← In large bowl, whisk together eggs, milk, mustard, salt and pepper. Add bread cubes, broccoli, 1 cup (250 mL) of the cheese and green onions; gently toss together. Spread in greased 13- x 9-inch glass baking dish; let stand for 30 minutes. *Make-ahead: Cover and refrigerate for up to 12 hours.*

← Sprinkle with remaining cheese. Bake in 375°F (190°C) oven until puffed and golden, 40 to 45 minutes. Sprinkle with parsley.

PER EACH OF 8 SERVINGS: about 346 cal, 19 g pro, 15 g total fat (7 g sat. fat), 33 g carb, 2 g fibre, 195 mg chol, 664 mg sodium. % RDI: 29% calcium, 19% iron, 23% vit A, 23% vit C, 38% folate.

DELI DELIGHT QUICHE

Quiche came, quiche went, and now it's back to a new generation. Handy pie shells make quiche a lot easier to prepare. No pressure to roll out pastry.

Makes 4 to 6 servings

1	deep 9-inch (23 cm) unbaked pie shell	1
3	eggs	3
1¼ cups	milk	300 mL
¼ tsp	each salt and pepper	1 mL
Pinch	nutmeg	Pinch
½ tsp	dried Italian herb seasoning	2 mL
FILLING		
2 oz	chopped salami, ham or smoked chicken	60 g
¾ cup	shredded provolone cheese	175 mL
¼ cup	each chopped black olives and roasted red pepper	50 mL

← Prick pie shell all over with fork. Line with foil; fill with pie weights or dried beans. Bake in bottom third of 400°F (200°C) oven until rim is light golden, about 15 minutes. Remove foil and weights. Place on rimmed baking sheet.

← **FILLING:** Sprinkle salami, cheese, olives and red pepper evenly over pie shell. In bowl, whisk together eggs, milk, salt, pepper and nutmeg; pour over filling. Sprinkle with herb seasoning.

← Bake in bottom third of 350°F (180°C) oven until knife inserted in centre comes out clean, about 50 minutes.

← 265

PER EACH OF 6 SERVINGS: about 270 cal, 11 g pro. 17 g total fat (7 g sat. fat), 17 g carb, 1 g fibre, 113 mg chol, 599 mg sodium. % RDI: 18% calcium 10% iron, 13% vit A, 22% vit C, 12% folate.

VARIATION

TURKEY QUICHE

Omit Filling. Use ⅓ cup (75 mL) diced smoked turkey or ham, ¾ cup (175 mL) shredded Jarlsberg cheese and ¼ cup (50 mL) each finely diced sweet red and green pepper. Substitute dried oregano for the Italian herb seasoning.

PASTA PRIMAVERA FRITTATA

Frittatas are delicious straight from the oven or at room temperature and keep well in the refrigerator for up to two days. Try a wedge in focaccia bread for a great sandwich.

Makes 4 servings

1 tbsp	vegetable oil	15 mL
1	onion, sliced	1
1	carrot, thinly sliced	1
2	cloves garlic, minced	2
½ tsp	dried Italian herb seasoning	2 mL
8	eggs	8
¼ cup	milk	50 mL
½ tsp	salt	2 mL
¼ tsp	pepper	1 mL
1 cup	cooked short pasta (about ¾ cup/175 mL uncooked)	250 mL
1½ cups	frozen broccoli florets, thawed	375 mL
Dash	hot pepper sauce	Dash
⅓ cup	grated Parmesan cheese	75 mL

⇐ 267

← In 9- or 10-inch (23 or 25 cm) nonstick ovenproof skillet, heat oil over medium heat; fry onion, carrot, garlic and herb seasoning, stirring often, until softened, 5 to 8 minutes.

← In large bowl, whisk together eggs, milk, salt and pepper; add pasta, broccoli and hot pepper sauce. Pour into skillet, stirring to combine.

← Sprinkle Parmesan cheese over egg mixture. Reduce heat to medium-low; cook until bottom and side are firm yet top is still slightly runny, about 10 minutes. Broil until golden and set, 3 to 5 minutes. Slice into wedges.

PER SERVING: about 305 cal, 20 g pro, 16 g total fat (5 g sat. fat), 19 g carb, 3 g fibre, 380 mg chol, 631 mg sodium. % RDI: 21% calcium, 15% iron, 73% vit A, 38% vit C, 41% folate.

SAUCY TOMATO POACHED EGGS

Served with buttery herbed panini rolls, this dish is a quick dinner as well as a terrific brunch item.

Makes 4 servings

1 tbsp	extra-virgin olive oil	15 mL
1	onion, chopped	1
1	zucchini, sliced	1
2	cloves garlic, sliced	2
1 tsp	dried Italian herb seasoning	5 mL
¼ tsp	each salt and pepper	1 mL
1	can (28 oz/796 mL) tomatoes	1
6	eggs	6

← In large skillet, heat oil over medium-high heat; fry onion, zucchini, garlic, herb seasoning, salt and pepper, stirring often, until onion is softened, about 5 minutes.

← Add tomatoes, breaking up with spoon; cook until thickened and most of the liquid is evaporated, about 20 minutes.

← Make 6 wells in sauce; gently break egg into each. Cover and cook until whites are set, about 5 minutes, or until desired doneness.

PER SERVING: about 202 cal, 12 g pro, 11 g total fat (3 g sat. fat), 14 g carb, 3 g fibre, 322 mg chol, 568 mg sodium. % RDI: 10% calcium, 19% iron, 27% vit A, 37% vit C, 21% folate.

HERBED PANINI

Garlic and herbs liven up bakery-fresh rolls.

Makes 4 servings

2 tbsp	butter, softened	25 mL
1	clove garlic, minced	1
2 tsp	chopped fresh parsley	10 mL
Pinch	dried oregano	Pinch
4	oval panini rolls	4

← In small bowl, mix together butter, garlic, parsley and oregano. Cut rolls in half horizontally; spread butter mixture onto cut sides. Close rolls and wrap in foil; bake in 400°F (200°C) oven until butter is melted, about 15 minutes.

PER SERVING: about 235 cal, 6 g pro, 8 g total fat (4 g sat. fat), 33 g carb, 4 g fibre, 16 mg chol, 399 mg sodium. % RDI: 6% calcium, 15% iron, 6% vit A, 2% vit C, 26% folate.

POLENTA WITH SAUTÉED SPINACH AND RED PEPPERS

You can substitute Swiss chard for the spinach in this vibrant gold, red and green comfort dish.

Makes 4 servings

½ tsp	salt	2 mL
1 cup	cornmeal	250 mL
2 tbsp	butter	25 mL
1 tbsp	extra-virgin olive oil	15 mL
Half	onion, finely chopped	Half
3	cloves garlic, thinly sliced	3
2	sweet red peppers, diced	2
½ tsp	each salt and pepper	2 mL
2	pkg (each 10 oz/284 g) fresh spinach, trimmed	2
½ cup	shredded old white Cheddar cheese	125 mL
1 cup	tomato-basil pasta sauce, heated	250 mL

← 271

← In large saucepan, bring 4 cups (1 L) water and salt to boil over high heat; reduce heat to low. Whisk in cornmeal; simmer, stirring almost constantly with wooden spoon, until thick enough to mound on spoon, about 15 minutes. Stir in butter. Pour into greased 8-inch (2 L) square glass baking dish, smoothing top with spatula. Place plastic wrap directly on surface; let cool. *Make-ahead: Refrigerate for up to 24 hours.*

← Meanwhile, in large skillet, heat oil over medium-high heat; fry onion, garlic, red peppers, salt and pepper stirring occasionally, until peppers are softened, about 4 minutes. Add spinach; cover and cook, stirring occasionally, until brightened and limp, about 4 minutes.

← Meanwhile, remove polenta from dish. Cut into quarters; cut each in half horizontally. Arrange on rimmed baking sheet. Top with spinach mixture, adding any juices from skillet; sprinkle with cheese. Broil until polenta is hot and cheese is bubbly, about 1 minute. Serve with pasta sauce.

PER SERVING: about 236 cal, 8 g pro, 11 g total fat (5 g sat. fat), 28 g carb, 5 g fibre, 22 mg chol, 717 mg sodium. % RDI: 19% calcium, 28% iron, 91% vit A, 128% vit C, 64% folate.

BAKED EGGPLANT WITH YOGURT SAUCE

Sweet tomato sauce and garlic-spiced yogurt top eggplant in this vegetarian dish that has its origins in Afghanistan.

Makes 8 servings

3	eggplants (total 3 lb/1.5 kg)	3
⅓ cup	extra-virgin olive oil or vegetable oil	75 mL
1 tsp	each salt and pepper	5 mL
1	onion, minced	1
1	can (28 oz/796 mL) diced tomatoes, drained	1
2 tbsp	tomato paste	25 mL
3 tbsp	chopped fresh parsley	50 mL
YOGURT SAUCE		
2	cloves garlic	2
½ tsp	salt	2 mL
1 cup	Balkan-style plain yogurt	250 mL
1 tsp	ground thyme	5 mL

← **YOGURT SAUCE:** On cutting board and using side of knife, mash garlic with salt until smooth paste forms. In bowl, whisk together yogurt, garlic paste and ½ tsp (2 mL) of the thyme. Set aside. *Make-ahead: Cover and refrigerate for up to 24 hours.*

← 273

← Cut eggplants into ½-inch (1 cm) thick rounds; arrange in single layer on foil-lined rimmed baking sheets.

← In small bowl, whisk ¼ cup (50 mL) of the oil with ½ tsp (2 mL) each of the salt and pepper; brush over eggplant. Broil about 8 inches (20 cm) from heat and turning once, until softened, browned and edges are wrinkled, about 20 minutes.

← Meanwhile, in large skillet, heat remaining oil over medium-high heat; fry onion, stirring occasionally, until golden, about 5 minutes. Add tomatoes, tomato paste and remaining salt and pepper; bring to boil. Reduce heat and simmer until liquid is evaporated and spoon drawn through sauce leaves gap, about 8 minutes.

← Arrange half of the eggplant in greased 13- x 9-inch (3 L) glass baking dish; top with 1 cup (250 mL) of the tomato sauce. Top with remaining eggplant then remaining tomato sauce. Sprinkle with 2 tbsp (25 mL) of the parsley. *Make-ahead: Cover and refrigerate for up to 24 hours.*

← Bake in 375°F (190°C) oven until bubbly, about 25 minutes. To serve, spoon yogurt sauce over eggplant. Sprinkle with remaining thyme and parsley.

PER SERVING: about 169 cal, 4 g pro, 10 g total fat (2 g sat. fat), 18 g carb, 5 g fibre, 3 mg chol, 556 mg sodium. % RDI 8% calcium, 10% iron, 7% vit A, 27% vit C, 16% folate.

VEGETARIAN TEX-MEX SHEPHERD'S PIE

274 →

Bulgur, either medium or coarse, adds a ground-beef type of texture to the sauce of this comfy casserole.

Makes 4 to 6 servings

6	Yukon Gold potatoes (about 2 lb/1 kg)	6
¼ cup	milk	50 mL
2 tbsp	chopped fresh parsley	25 mL
2 tbsp	butter	25 mL
¾ tsp	each salt and pepper	4 mL
1 tbsp	vegetable oil	15 mL
2	carrots, diced	2
1	each onion and sweet red pepper, chopped	1
1 tbsp	chili powder	15 mL
½ tsp	ground cumin	2 mL
Pinch	cayenne pepper	Pinch
¾ cup	bulgur	175 mL
2 tbsp	all-purpose flour	25 mL
1½ cups	vegetable stock	375 mL
1 cup	corn kernels	250 mL

← Peel and cut potatoes into 2-inch (5 cm) chunks. In saucepan of boiling salted water, cover and cook potatoes until tender, about 20 minutes; drain and mash. Blend in milk, parsley, butter and ½ tsp (2 mL) each of the salt and pepper.

← Meanwhile, in large skillet, heat oil over medium heat; fry carrots, onion, red pepper, chili powder, cumin and cayenne pepper, stirring occasionally, until onion is softened, about 5 minutes.

← Add bulgur and flour; cook, stirring, for 1 minute. Gradually stir in stock; cover and cook over low heat until liquid is absorbed, about 10 minutes.

← Add corn and remaining salt and pepper. Spread in 8-inch (2 L) square glass baking dish; spread potatoes over top. Broil for 2 minutes or until golden. *Make-ahead: Let cool for 30 minutes; refrigerate until cold. Cover and refrigerate for up to 24 hours; reheat, covered, in 350°F (180°C) oven for 30 minutes or until filling is bubbly.*

PER EACH OF 6 SERVINGS: about 277 cal, 7 g pro, 7 g total fat (3 g sat. fat), 50 g carb, 6 g fibre, 11 mg chol, 529 mg sodium.

% RDI: 5% calcium, 14% iron, 78% vit A, 73% vit C, 19% folate.

PAN-FRIED TOFU WITH ASIAN GARLIC SAUCE

Tofu is good, but with a zesty ginger and garlic sauce, it's even better. Serve this with brown rice and the quick Sesame Green Bean Stir-Fry (recipe, opposite).

Makes 4 servings

1	pkg (350 g) extra-firm tofu	1
2 tbsp	vegetable oil	25 mL
1	onion, chopped	1
3	cloves garlic, minced	3
1 tsp	minced gingerroot (or ½ tsp/2 mL ground)	5 mL
¼ tsp	pepper	1 mL
¾ cup	vegetable stock or low-sodium chicken stock	175 mL
¼ cup	soy sauce	50 mL
1 tbsp	cornstarch	15 mL
2	green onions, sliced diagonally	2

← Pat tofu dry; cut crosswise into 4 slices. In large nonstick skillet, heat half of the oil over medium-high heat; fry tofu, turning once, until golden, about 8 minutes. Transfer to plates and keep warm.

← Add remaining oil to pan; fry onion, garlic, ginger and pepper over medium heat, stirring occasionally, until onion is softened, about 3 minutes.

← Add stock and soy sauce; bring to boil. Stir cornstarch with 1 tbsp (15 mL) water; stir into pan and boil, stirring, until thickened, about 1 minute. Pour over tofu. Sprinkle with onions.

PER SERVING: about 181 cal, 11 g pro, 12 g total fat (1 g sat. fat), 9 g carb, 1 g fibre, 0 mg chol, 1,155 mg sodium. % RDI: 13% calcium, 15% iron, 7% vit C, 15% folate.

SESAME GREEN BEAN STIR-FRY

This stir-fry/steam technique works with chopped asparagus and sugar snap peas, too.

← 277

Makes 4 servings

1 tsp	vegetable oil	5 mL
1 lb	green beans, trimmed	500 g
1 tsp	sesame seeds	5 mL
1 tsp	sesame oil	5 mL

← In skillet, heat oil over medium-high heat; stir-fry green beans for 2 minutes. Add 1 tbsp (15 mL) water, sesame seeds and sesame oil; cover and steam until beans are tender-crisp, about 4 minutes.

PER SERVING: about 59 cal, 2 g pro, 3 g total fat (trace sat. fat), 8 g carb, 2 g fibre, 0 mg cho , 3 mg sodium. % RDI: 4% calcium, 9% iron, 7% vit A, 15% vit C, 15% folate.

TOFU AND VEGETABLE SKEWERS WITH PEANUT SAUCE

These skewers are lovely with rice — whole grain or brown is always the healthiest choice. Use a grill pan, indoor grill or broiler when our Canadian weather is too hostile to barbecue outside.

Makes 4 servings

1	pkg (350 g) extra-firm tofu	1
2 cups	snow peas, trimmed	500 mL
2 cups	cherry tomatoes	500 mL
2 cups	small mushrooms	500 mL
2 tbsp	extra-virgin olive oil	25 mL
¼ tsp	each salt and pepper	1 mL
2	green onions, sliced	2

PEANUT SAUCE

½ cup	smooth peanut butter	125 mL
¼ cup	soy sauce	50 mL
2 tbsp	ketchup	25 mL
2 tbsp	lemon juice	25 mL
2	cloves garlic, minced	2

PEANUT SAUCE: In bowl, whisk together peanut butter, ½ cup (125 mL) warm water, soy sauce, ketchup, lemon juice and garlic. Remove ¾ cup (175 mL) and set aside. 279

Pat tofu dry. Cut in half horizontally; cut in half lengthwise. Cut crosswise 5 times for a total of 24 pieces; add to peanut sauce in bowl. Toss gently to coat; let stand for 10 minutes. Thread onto 4 soaked wooden or metal skewers.

Meanwhile, in separate bowl, toss together snow peas, tomatoes, mushrooms, oil, salt and pepper. Alternately thread vegetables onto 8 skewers.

Place vegetable and tofu skewers on greased grill over medium-high heat. Close lid and grill, turning once, until tofu is browned and vegetables are tender-crisp, about 10 minutes. To serve, drizzle with reserved peanut sauce; sprinkle with onions.

PER SERVING: about 303 cal, 17 g pro, 22 g total fat (4 g sat. fat), 15 g carb, 4 g fibre, 0 mg chol, 908 mg sodium. % RDI: 15% calcium, 26% iron, 8% vit A, 50% vit C, 29% folate.

TIP

If using wooden or bamboo skewers, soak them in water for 30 minutes before using to prevent scorching.

282 →

CHAPTER 8

S
OKIES

NO-BAKE CHOCOLATE MARBLE CHEESECAKE PIE

Because this creamy cheesecake doesn't require baking, it will consistently turn out delicious and beautiful, with no cracks.

Makes 8 to 10 servings

1½ cups	chocolate wafer crumbs	375 mL
⅓ cup	butter, melted	75 mL
FILLING		
4 oz	bittersweet chocolate, finely chopped	125 g
¾ cup	whipping cream	175 mL
12 oz	cream cheese, softened	375 g
⅓ cup	sweetened condensed milk	75 mL
1 tsp	vanilla	5 mL
TOPPING		
¾ cup	whipping cream	175 mL
1 oz	bittersweet chocolate, finely chopped	30 g

← In bowl, stir crumbs with butter until moistened; press onto bottom and up side of 9-inch (23 cm) pie plate. Refrigerate until firm, about 30 minutes. ← 287

← **FILLING:** Place chocolate in heatproof bowl. In small saucepan, heat half of the cream just until boiling; pour over chocolate, whisking until melted. Let cool slightly.

← In separate bowl, beat together cream cheese, remaining cream, condensed milk and vanilla until smooth; spoon into prepared crust, leaving gaps between spoonfuls. Pour chocolate mixture into gaps. With tip of knife, swirl mixtures together roughly. Tap on counter to smooth top. Cover and refrigerate until firm, about 4 hours. *Make-ahead: Refrigerate for up to 2 days.*

← **TOPPING:** In bowl, whip cream; spoon into piping bag and pipe into rosettes on pie. Sprinkle chopped chocolate over cream.

PER EACH OF 10 SERVINGS: about 482 cal, 7 g pro, 43 g total fat (26 g sat. fat), 24 g carb, 3 g fibre, 110 mg chol, 299 mg sodium. % RDI: 9% calcium, 13% iron, 35% vit A, 8% folate.

TIP

No piping bag? No problem. You can garnish the pie with spoonfuls of whipped cream then chopped chocolate.

BUTTERSCOTCH APPLE SPICE CAKE

No celebration would be complete without a finale. Serve this fine cake with whipped cream, crème fraîche or a slice of Stilton or Bénédictin cheese if you favour a little savoury with your sweets.

Makes 12 servings

¼ cup	butter, softened	50 mL
½ cup	granulated sugar	125 mL
⅓ cup	packed brown sugar	75 mL
2	eggs	2
1 tsp	vanilla	5 mL
⅔ cup	sour cream	150 mL
¼ cup	apple juice or cider	50 mL
1¾ cups	all-purpose flour	425 mL
2 tbsp	chopped crystallized ginger	25 mL
1½ tsp	each baking powder and cinnamon	7 mL
½ tsp	baking soda	2 mL
¼ tsp	each ground nutmeg and salt	1 mL
¼ tsp	aniseeds, crushed	1 mL
TOPPING		
¾ cup	packed brown sugar	175 mL
¼ cup	butter	50 mL
2	apples, peeled and sliced	2

← 289

← Line bottom of 10-inch (4 L) tube pan with parchment or waxed paper; set aside.

← In bowl, beat together butter, granulated sugar and brown sugar until combined. Beat in eggs, 1 at a time; beat in vanilla. Whisk sour cream with apple juice; set aside.

← In separate bowl, whisk together flour, ginger, baking powder, cinnamon, baking soda, nutmeg, salt and aniseeds; stir into butter mixture alternately with sour cream mixture, making 3 additions of dry ingredients and 2 of sour cream. Scrape into prepared pan.

← **TOPPING:** In small saucepan, heat sugar with butter over medium heat until bubbly. Arrange apples attractively over batter; drizzle with butter mixture. Bake in centre of 375°F (190°C) oven until tester inserted in centre comes out clean, about 45 minutes.

PER SERVING: about 278 cal, 3 g pro, 11 g total fat (6 g sat. fat), 44 g carb, 1 g fibre, 62 mg chol, 231 mg sodium. % RDI: 6% calcium, 12% iron, 10% vit A, 5% vit C, 8% folate.

TIP

Use a mortar and pestle to crush aniseeds. Or place seeds in a sturdy bag and crush under a heavy pot or skillet.

CHOCOLATE PEANUT BUTTER PIE

290 →

This irresistible combination has it all — a crunchy crust, a creamy rich filling, a velvety ganache and a sprinkle of peanuts.

Makes 8 servings

1½ cups	chocolate wafer crumbs	375 mL
⅓ cup	butter, melted	75 mL
FILLING		
½ cup	whipping cream	125 mL
1	pkg (8 oz/250 g) cream cheese, cubed	1
1 cup	smooth peanut butter	250 mL
2 tbsp	butter, softened	25 mL
1 tbsp	vanilla	15 mL
1 cup	icing sugar	250 mL
TOPPING		
6 oz	bittersweet or semisweet chocolate	175 g
½ cup	whipping cream	125 mL
2 tbsp	chopped roasted peanuts	25 mL

← In bowl, toss crumbs with butter. Pat into 9-inch (23 cm) pie plate, without covering rim. Bake in centre of 350°F (180°C) oven until firm, about 8 minutes. Let cool.

← FILLING: In bowl, whip cream; set aside. In large bowl, beat cream cheese until smooth; beat in peanut butter, butter and vanilla. Beat in icing sugar until fluffy. Fold in one-quarter of the whipped cream; fold in remaining cream. Spread over crust. Cover loosely and refrigerate until firm, about 2 hours.

← TOPPING: Meanwhile, finely chop chocolate; place in heatproof bowl. In small saucepan, warm cream over medium-low heat until bubbles form around edge; pour over chocolate and stir until melted. Let cool. Drizzle over filling; sprinkle with nuts.

← Cover loosely and refrigerate until set, about 2 hours. *Make-ahead: Refrigerate for up to 2 days.*

PER SERVING: about 756 cal, 15 g pro, 64 g total fat (31 g sat. fat), 43 g carb, 5 g fibre, 101 mg chol, 494 mg sodium. % RDI: 8% calcium, 23% iron, 34% vit A, 16% folate.

RASPBERRY STREUSEL COFFEE CAKE

Put a taste of summer on your morning table. If using frozen raspberries, buy unsweetened individually quick frozen (IQF) berries; do not thaw to use, and bake for 5 to 10 minutes longer.

Makes 10 to 12 servings

½ cup	butter, softened	125 mL
1 cup	granulated sugar	250 mL
2	eggs	2
1 tsp	vanilla	5 mL
2 cups	all-purpose flour	500 mL
1 tsp	each baking powder and baking soda	5 mL
½ tsp	salt	2 mL
1 cup	sour cream	250 mL
3 cups	fresh or frozen raspberries	750 mL

STREUSEL TOPPING

1½ cups	all-purpose flour	375 mL
½ cup	finely chopped pecans	125 mL
⅓ cup	packed brown sugar	75 mL
⅓ cup	granulated sugar	75 mL
½ cup	butter	125 mL

CREAM CHEESE FILLING

1	pkg (250 g) cream cheese, softened	1
¼ cup	granulated sugar	50 mL
1	egg	1
2 tsp	finely grated lemon rind	10 mL

← Grease 13- x 9-inch (3.5 L) metal cake pan; set aside.

← 293

← **STREUSEL TOPPING:** In bowl, combine flour, pecans, brown sugar and granulated sugar. Using pastry blender or 2 knives, cut in butter until crumbly. Set aside.

← **CREAM CHEESE FILLING:** In bowl, beat cream cheese with sugar until fluffy; beat in egg and lemon rind. Set aside

← In large bowl, beat butter with sugar until light and fluffy. Beat in eggs, 1 at a time, beating well after each addition; beat in vanilla. In separate bowl, whisk together flour, baking powder, baking soda and salt; stir into butter mixture alternately with sour cream, making 3 additions of dry ingredients and 2 of sour cream.

← Spread in prepared pan; sprinkle raspberries over top Gently spread with cream cheese filling; sprinkle evenly with streusel topping.

← Bake in centre of 350°F (180°C) oven until tester inserted in centre comes out clean, 45 to 50 minutes. Serve warm or at room temperature.

PER EACH OF 12 SERVINGS: about 562 cal, 8 g pro, 30 g total fat (17 g sat. fat). 66 g carb, 3 g fibre, 125 mg chol, 459 mg sodium.
% RDI: 7% calcium, 17% iron, 28% vit A, 10% vit C, 25% folate.

HARVEST STREUSEL COFFEE CAKE

In the summer, Canadian peaches, nectarines or plums are the finest choice. However, for year-round enjoyment, there are always apples and ripe juicy pears to stud the top of this moist cake.

Makes 10 to 12 servings

4	ripe peaches (about 1¼ lb/625 g)	4
¾ cup	butter, softened	175 mL
1½ cups	granulated sugar	375 mL
3	eggs	3
1½ tsp	vanilla	7 mL
3 cups	all-purpose flour	750 mL
1½ tsp	each baking powder and baking soda	7 mL
1½ tsp	ground ginger	7 mL
¾ tsp	salt	4 mL
1½ cups	sour cream	375 mL
STREUSEL		
⅓ cup	packed brown sugar	75 mL
¼ cup	all-purpose flour	50 mL
¼ cup	chopped almonds	50 mL
2 tbsp	finely chopped crystallized ginger	25 mL
2 tbsp	cold butter, diced	25 mL

← Grease 13- x 9-inch (3.5 L) metal cake pan; set aside.

← Peel peaches; cut in half and remove pits. Place, cut side down, on cutting board; slice thinly. Set aside.

← In large bowl, beat butter with sugar until light and fluffy. Beat in eggs, 1 at a time, beating well after each addition; beat in vanilla. In separate bowl, whisk together flour, baking powder, baking soda, ginger and salt; stir into butter mixture alternately with sour cream, making 3 additions of dry ingredients and 2 of sour cream. Spread in prepared pan. Without overlapping, arrange fruit attractively over top.

← **STREUSEL:** In bowl, mix together sugar, flour, almonds and ginger. With pastry blender or 2 knives, cut in butter until crumbly; sprinkle evenly over fruit.

← Bake in centre of 350°F (180°C) oven until cake tester inserted in centre comes out clean, about 1 hour. Let cool in pan on rack.

← 295

PER EACH OF 12 SERVINGS: about 466 cal, 7 g pro, 20 g total fat (11 g sat. fat), 65 g carb, 2 g fibre, 101 mg chol, 492 mg sodium. % RDI: 7% calcium, 17% iron, 20% vit A, 5% vit C, 20% folate.

VARIATIONS

PLUM STREUSEL COFFEE CAKE
Use 2 cups (500 mL) sliced pitted (unpeeled) plums instead of peaches. Use 1 tsp (5 mL) cinnamon or ½ tsp (2 mL) nutmeg instead of ground ginger. Omit crystallized ginger.

NECTARINE STREUSEL COFFEE CAKE
Substitute 2 cups (500 mL) sliced pitted (unpeeled) nectarines for the peaches.

PUMPKIN CUPCAKES WITH CREAM CHEESE ICING

296 →

Perky little spiced cupcakes are a lunchbox treat.

Makes 12 cupcakes

2 cups	all-purpose flour	**500 mL**
1 cup	granulated sugar	**250 mL**
1½ tsp	each pumpkin pie spice and baking powder	**7 mL**
1 tsp	baking soda	**5 mL**
½ tsp	salt	**2 mL**
2	eggs	**2**
1 cup	canned pumpkin	**250 mL**
½ cup	buttermilk	**125 mL**
¼ cup	vegetable oil	**50 mL**
ICING		
1	pkg (250 g) cream cheese, softened	**1**
1 tbsp	butter, softened	**15 mL**
1 tsp	vanilla	**5 mL**
1 cup	icing sugar	**250 mL**
	Orange or coloured sprinkles (optional)	

← In large bowl, whisk together flour, sugar, pie spice, baking powder, baking soda and salt. In separate bowl, whisk eggs; whisk in pumpkin, buttermilk and oil. Pour over dry ingredients; stir just until moistened.

← Spoon into large paper-lined muffin cups, filling to top. Bake in centre of 375°F (190°C) oven until cake tester inserted in centre comes out clean, about 25 minutes. Let cool on rack.

← **ICING:** In bowl, beat together cream cheese, butter and vanilla; beat in sugar until smooth. Spread on cupcakes. Decorate with sprinkles (if using).

PER CUPCAKE: about 320 cal, 5 g pro, 14 g total fat (6 g sat. fat), 44 g carb, 1 g fibre, 57 mg chol, 319 mg sodium. % RDI: 5% calcium, 12% iron, 51% vit A, 2% vit C, 16% folate.

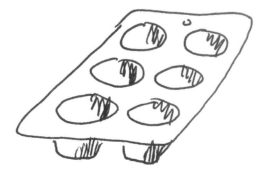

PEACH AND BERRY COBBLER

A golden biscuit topping blankets the juicy filling in this old-fashioned but never-out-of-fashion dessert.

Makes 8 servings

6 cups	sliced peeled peaches or nectarines	**1.5 L**
1 cup	raspberries or blueberries	**250 mL**
⅓ cup	granulated sugar	**75 mL**
2 tbsp	all-purpose flour	**25 mL**
1 tbsp	lemon juice	**15 mL**
BUTTERMILK BISCUIT TOPPING		
1½ cups	all-purpose flour	**375 mL**
¼ cup	granulated sugar	**50 mL**
2 tsp	grated lemon rind	**10 mL**
1 tsp	baking powder	**5 mL**
¼ tsp	baking soda	**1 mL**
Pinch	salt	**Pinch**
¼ cup	cold butter, cubed	**50 mL**
⅔ cup	buttermilk	**150 mL**
1 tsp	vanilla	**5 mL**
GARNISH		
2 tbsp	buttermilk	**25 mL**
1 tsp	granulated sugar	**5 mL**

← In large bowl, gently toss together peaches, raspberries, sugar, flour and lemon juice; scrape into 8-inch (2 L) square glass baking dish.

← **BUTTERMILK BISCUIT TOPPING:** In large bowl, whisk together flour, sugar, lemon rind, baking powder, baking soda and salt. Using pastry blender or 2 knives, cut in butter until crumbly. In measuring cup, stir buttermilk with vanilla; drizzle over flour mixture, stirring with fork to form soft slightly sticky dough.

← Turn out onto lightly floured waxed paper; form into 8-inch (20 cm) square. Cut into 9 squares; place over fruit.

← **GARNISH:** Brush squares with buttermilk; sprinkle with sugar. Bake in 375°F (190°C) oven until bubbly and biscuits are light golden and no longer doughy underneath when lifted with spoon, about 50 minutes. Let cool on rack. *Make-ahead: Cover loosely with foil and refrigerate for up to 24 hours; reheat, covered, in 350°F (180°C) oven for about 30 minutes.*

PER SERVING: about 278 cal, 5 g pro, 6 g total fat (4 g sat. fat), 53 g carb, 3 g fibre, 16 mg chol, 155 mg sodium. % RDI: 5% calcium, 9% iron, 11% vit A, 15% vit C, 15% folate.

PEAR GINGERBREAD PUDDING

There's sheer comfort in a bowl of this layered pudding. Add a scoop of frozen vanilla yogurt to turn contentment into bliss.

Makes 6 servings

2	large pears, peeled, cored and cubed	2
2 tbsp	liquid honey	25 mL
GINGERBREAD TOPPING		
½ cup	butter, softened	125 mL
½ cup	granulated sugar	125 mL
¼ cup	fancy molasses	50 mL
1	egg	1
¾ cup	all-purpose flour	175 mL
1 tsp	each ground ginger and cinnamon	5 mL
½ tsp	baking soda	2 mL
¼ tsp	ground cloves	1 mL
Pinch	salt	Pinch
⅔ cup	hot water	150 mL

◄ 301

← Grease 8-inch (2 L) square glass baking dish. Spread pears in dish; drizzle with honey. Set aside.

← **GINGERBREAD TOPPING:** In large bowl, beat butter with sugar until fluffy; beat in molasses and egg until combined. In separate bowl, whisk together flour, ginger, cinnamon, baking soda, cloves and salt; stir into molasses mixture alternately with hot water, making 3 additions of dry ingredients and 2 of water. Pour over pears.

← Bake in centre of 350°F (180°C) oven until cake tester inserted in centre of cake part comes out clean, about 30 minutes. Serve warm.

PER SERVING: about 357 cal, 3 g pro, 17 g total fat (10 g sat. fat), 51 g carb, 2 g fibre, 79 mg chol, 271 mg sodium.% RDI: 5% calcium, 13% iron, 15% vit A, 3% vit C, 12% folate.

RASPBERRY PUDDING

This pudding tastes as sensational as it looks. The recipe comes from Le Lapin Sauté, a charming restaurant in Quebec City.

Makes 8 servings

2	pkg (each 300 g) frozen raspberries, thawed	2
½ cup	granulated sugar	125 mL
CAKE TOPPING		
½ cup	butter, softened	125 mL
¾ cup	granulated sugar	175 mL
2	eggs	2
½ tsp	vanilla	2 mL
1¼ cups	all-purpose flour	300 mL
1½ tsp	baking powder	7 mL
Pinch	salt	Pinch
½ cup	milk	125 mL

← Drain raspberries, reserving juice in measure; add enough water to make 1 cup (250 mL). Set aside.

← In greased 8-inch (2 L) square metal cake pan, toss raspberries with ¼ cup (50 mL) of the sugar; set aside.

← **CAKE TOPPING:** In large bowl, beat butter with sugar until light and fluffy. Beat in eggs, 1 at a time; beat in vanilla. In separate bowl, whisk together flour, baking powder and salt; add to butter mixture alternately with milk, making 3 additions of flour mixture and 2 of milk. Scrape evenly over raspberries, smoothing top. Set aside.

← In small saucepan, bring reserved raspberry juice and remaining sugar to boil; pour over batter. Bake in centre of 350°F (180°C) oven until edges are bubbly and cake is firm to the touch, about 50 minutes. Let cool slightly before serving. *Make-ahead: Store at room temperature for up to 8 hours; reheat if desired.*

PER SERVING: about 357 cal, 5 g pro, 14 g total fat (8 g sat. fat), 56 g carb, 4 g fibre, 86 mg chol, 190 mg sodium. % RDI: 6% calcium, 11% iron, 15% vit A, 23% vit C, 16% folate.

THREE–ICE CREAM TERRINE WITH MOCHA SAUCE

Customize this layered terrine, a stunning yet simple-to-make dessert, with your favourite ice-cream flavours. It helps to soften the ice cream for about 20 minutes in the refrigerator before layering it in the pan.

Makes 12 servings

2 cups	cubed (½ inch/1 cm) brownies	500 mL
2 cups	softened chocolate ice cream	500 mL
2 cups	softened coffee ice cream	500 mL
2 cups	softened vanilla ice cream	500 mL

MOCHA SAUCE

1 tbsp	instant coffee granules	15 mL
⅓ cup	water	75 mL
⅓ cup	granulated sugar	75 mL
⅓ cup	corn syrup	75 mL
½ cup	whipping cream	125 mL
6 oz	bittersweet chocolate, chopped	175 g

Line 8- x 4-inch (1.5 L) loaf pan with plastic wrap, leaving 3-inch (8 cm) overhang. Gently pack half of the brownies evenly over pan. Spread with chocolate ice cream, smoothing top; freeze until firm, about 2 hours.

Spread coffee ice cream over chocolate ice cream, smoothing top; freeze until firm, about 2 hours.

Spread vanilla ice cream over coffee ice cream, smoothing top. Sprinkle with remaining brownies; press in gently. Fold plastic overhang over top; freeze until firm, about 2 hours *Make-ahead: Overwrap with heavy-duty foil; freeze for up to 1 week.*

MOCHA SAUCE: In small saucepan, dissolve coffee granules in water; add sugar and corn syrup. Bring to boil; cook, stirring, for 1 minute. Add cream and chocolate; cook, stirring, over medium heat until smooth, about 2 minutes. Let cool. *Make-ahead: Refrigerate in airtight container for up to 1 week; to reheat, microwave at medium-high for 1 minute.*

Turn out terrine onto chilled serving plate, removing plastic wrap. Let stand in refrigerator until soft enough to slice, about 15 minutes. Serve with mocha sauce.

PER SERVING: about 297 cal, 4 g pro, 19 g total fat (11 g sat. fat), 35 g carb, 3 g fibre 37 mg chol, 76 mg sodium. % RDI: 9% calcium, 10% iron, 14% vit A, 5% vit C, 6% folate.

VARIATION

THREE ICE–CREAM TERRINE WITH CHOCOLATE FUDGE SAUCE

Omit instant coffee granules.

BAKED FUDGE DESSERT

"This moist cake, which was in my grandma's recipe file, is an updated version of an heirloom recipe that dates back more than 100 years," says Ruth Lee of Troy, Ont. The Canadian Living Test Kitchen declared this version of the two-layer chocolate dessert — with cake on top and sauce on the bottom — the best they have ever tasted.

Makes 6 servings

1 cup	sifted cake-and-pastry flour	250 mL
½ cup	granulated sugar	125 mL
3 tbsp	cocoa powder	50 mL
2 tsp	baking powder	10 mL
½ tsp	salt	2 mL
½ cup	chopped nuts	125 mL
½ cup	milk	125 mL
2 tbsp	butter, melted	25 mL
1 tsp	vanilla	5 mL
SAUCE		
1¾ cups	hot water	425 mL
½ cup	packed brown sugar	125 mL
¼ cup	cocoa powder	50 mL

← Grease 8-inch (2 L) square glass baking dish; set aside.

← In bowl, whisk together flour, sugar, cocoa powder, baking powder and salt; stir in nuts. Add milk, butter and vanilla; stir just until smooth. Scrape into prepared dish.

← **SAUCE:** In separate bowl, whisk together hot water, sugar and cocoa powder; pour over batter. Bake in centre of 350°F (180°C) oven until bubbly around edges and cake springs back when lightly touched, about 35 minutes. Serve warm.

PER SERVING: about 325 cal, 5 g pro, 12 g total fat (4 g sat. fat), 55 g carb, 3 g fibre, 12 mg chol, 337 mg sodium. % RDI: 9% calcium, 21% iron, 5% vit A, 13% folate.

CARAMEL PECAN BROWNIES

The mix of bittersweet and unsweetened chocolate gives these supremely decadent brownies a nice little edge.

Makes 16 pieces

1	roll (52 g) soft caramel-and-milk-chocolate candy (such as Rolo or Caramilk)	1
4 oz	bittersweet or semisweet chocolate, chopped	125 g
2 oz	unsweetened chocolate, chopped	60 g
½ cup	butter, cubed	125 mL
1 cup	granulated sugar	250 mL
1 tsp	vanilla	5 mL
2	eggs	2
¾ cup	all-purpose flour	175 mL
½ cup	chopped toasted pecans	125 mL
¼ tsp	baking powder	1 mL
Pinch	salt	Pinch
2 tbsp	butterscotch sauce	25 mL

← Line 8-inch (2 L) square metal cake pan with parchment paper, leaving overhang for handles. Set aside.

← Cut each caramel chocolate candy into quarters; set aside.

← 309

← In heavy saucepan, melt together bittersweet and unsweetened chocolates and butter over low heat, stirring; let cool slightly. Whisk in sugar and vanilla; whisk in eggs, 1 at a time, until shiny.

← In bowl, whisk together flour, half of the pecans, the baking powder and salt; gently stir into chocolate mixture just until combined. Scrape into prepared pan. Drizzle with half of the butterscotch sauce. Scatter remaining pecans and caramel chocolate candy over top, lightly pressing into batter without submerging. Drizzle with remaining sauce.

← Bake in centre of 350°F (180°C) oven until tester inserted in centre comes out clean, about 35 minutes. Let cool in pan on rack. Using handles, lift out of pan; trim edges and cut into squares. *Make-ahead: Wrap in foil and store at room temperature for up to 5 days or freeze in airtight container for up to 1 month.*

PER PIECE: about 236 cal, 3 g pro, 15 g total fat (7 g sat. fat), 26 g carb, 2 g fibre, 45 mg chol, 83 mg sodium. % RDI: 2% calcium, 8% iron, 7% vit A, 3% folate.

TIP

Nonstick foil is an alternative to parchment paper when lining cake pans.

CHOCOLATE FONDUE

Fondue forks may be de rigueur at a fondue party, but small skewers or toothpicks make dipping the chunks of Mini Almond Cakes (recipe, this page) easier and neater. The fondue stays soft enough for dipping for up to an hour; if it begins to set, microwave it at high for 15 to 20 seconds.

Makes 2 cups (500 mL)

6 oz	bittersweet chocolate, finely chopped	**175 g**
4 oz	milk chocolate, finely chopped	**125 g**
¾ cup	whipping cream	**175 mL**
2 tbsp	amaretto, brandy or rum (optional)	**25 mL**

← Place bittersweet and milk chocolates in shallow heatproof glass bowl. In saucepan, bring cream to boil; pour over chocolate, whisking until melted. Whisk in amaretto (if using).

PER 1 TBSP (15 mL): about 64 cal, 1 g pro, 6 g total fat (4 g sat. fat), 4 g carb, 1 g fibre, 8 mg chol, 6 mg sodium. % RDI: 1% calcium, 3% iron, 2% vit A.

MINI ALMOND CAKES

← 311

These little cakes are firm enough to dip into the chocolate fondue. Cut into halves to encourage one dip, one bite.

Makes 15 cakes

¼ cup	butter, softened	**50 mL**
½ cup	granulated sugar	**125 mL**
2	eggs	**2**
¼ tsp	almond extract	**1 mL**
¾ cup	sifted cake-and-pastry flour	**175 mL**
2 tbsp	sliced almonds	**25 mL**

← Grease and flour mini muffin cups; set aside.
← In bowl, beat butter with sugar until fluffy; beat in eggs, 1 at a time. Beat in almond extract. Add flour; stir just until blended. Spoon into prepared cups. Press almonds onto tops.
← Bake in centre of 350°F (180°C) oven until cake tester inserted in centre comes out clean, about 15 minutes. Let cool in pan on rack for 5 minutes. Turn out onto rack; let cool completely. *Make-ahead: Layer between waxed paper and store in airtight container for up to 2 days or freeze for up to 2 weeks.*

PER CAKE: about 82 cal, 1 g pro, 4 g total fat (2 g sat. fat), 10 g carb, trace fibre, 32 mg chol, 37 mg sodium. % RDI: 1% calcium, 4% iron, 4% vit A, 4% folate.

CHOCOLATE PECAN OATMEAL COOKIES

312 →

Oatmeal cookies come in many flavours — all worth making. These use dark chocolate chips and pecans, but keep currants, walnuts, hazelnuts, dried cranberries and white chocolate chips in mind when it comes time to bake up another batch.

Makes about 36 cookies

⅔ cup	butter, softened	**150 mL**
1 cup	packed brown sugar	**250 mL**
1	egg	**1**
1 tsp	grated orange rind	**5 mL**
1½ cups	rolled oats (not instant)	**375 mL**
1 cup	all-purpose flour	**250 mL**
½ tsp	each baking powder and baking soda	**2 mL**
¼ tsp	salt	**1 mL**
¾ cup	chocolate chips	**175 mL**
½ cup	chopped pecans	**125 mL**

← Grease or line rimless baking sheet with parchment paper; set aside.

← In large bowl, beat butter with brown sugar until fluffy; beat in egg and orange rind. In separate bowl, mix together rolled oats, flour, baking powder, baking soda and salt; add to butter mixture and stir until blended. Stir in chocolate chips and pecans.

← Drop by heaping 1 tbsp (15 mL), about 2 inches (5 cm) apart, onto prepared pans. Bake in top and bottom thirds of 375°F (190°C) oven, rotating and switching pans halfway through, until golden, about 10 minutes. Let cool on pans on rack for 2 minutes. Transfer to rack; let cool completely.

PER COOKIE: about 110 cal, 1 g pro, 6 g total fat (3 g sat. fat), 13 g carb, 1 g fibre, 16 mg chol, 75 mg sodium. % RDI: 1% calcium, 4% iron, 4% vit A, 4% folate.

VARIATION

CLASSIC OATMEAL COOKIES

Substitute 1 tbsp (15 mL) vanilla and 1 tsp (5 mL) cinnamon for the orange rind. Substitute 1 cup (250 mL) raisins for the chocolate chips and pecans.

TRIPLE CHOCOLATE COOKIES

These intensely chocolaty cookies are just the thing when you want a chocolate fix. Team them up with your beverage of choice: milk, tea, chai or cappuccino.

Makes 48 cookies

1 cup	butter	250 mL
1 cup	granulated sugar	250 mL
½ cup	packed brown sugar	125 mL
2	eggs	2
1 tsp	vanilla	5 mL
2 cups	all-purpose flour	500 mL
½ cup	cocoa powder	125 mL
1 tsp	baking soda	5 mL
¼ tsp	salt	1 mL
1 cup	semisweet chocolate chips	250 mL
1 cup	white chocolate or milk chocolate chips	250 mL

← Line rimless baking sheets with parchment paper or nonstick foil, or grease; set aside.

← In large bowl, beat butter with granulated and brown sugars until fluffy. Beat in eggs, 1 at a time; beat in vanilla. In separate bowl, whisk together flour, cocoa, baking soda and salt; add to butter mixture, stirring to combine. Stir in semisweet and white chocolate chips.

← Drop by heaping 1 tbsp (15 mL), about 2 inches (5 cm) apart, onto prepared baking sheets. Bake in top and bottom thirds of 350°F (180°C) oven, rotating and switching pans halfway through, until firm to the touch and no longer glossy, about 12 minutes. Transfer to racks; let cool completely. *Make-ahead: Layer between waxed paper in airtight container and store for up to 5 days or freeze for up to 2 weeks.*

← 315

PER COOKIE: about 120 cal, 1 g pro, 6 g total fat (4 g sat. fat), 15 g carb, 1 g fibre, 21 mg chol, 82 mg sodium. % RDI: 1% calcium, 4% iron, 4% vit A, 4% folate.

~❧~

VARIATION

DOUBLE CHOCOLATE COOKIES
Replace cocoa powder with ½ cup (125 mL) all-purpose flour.

TIP

When baking cookies, there are three choices for lining pans: parchment paper, nonstick foil and silicone baking mats. They all work to ensure that every cookie bakes evenly.

~❧~

OATMEAL ENERGY BARS

Everyone needs a little energy to get through the day. Chewy and nutty, these bars will satisfy any sweet cravings as well as deliver a delicious pick-me-up.

Makes 12 bars

2⁄3 cup	butter, softened	150 mL
1 cup	packed brown sugar	250 mL
1	egg	1
1 tsp	vanilla	5 mL
1½ cups	rolled oats (not instant)	375 mL
1 cup	all-purpose flour	250 mL
½ tsp	each baking powder and baking soda	2 mL
¼ tsp	salt	1 mL
½ cup	chopped dried apricots	125 mL
½ cup	slivered almonds	125 mL
½ cup	dried cranberries	125 mL
½ cup	sweetened shredded coconut	125 mL

← Grease or line 13- x 9-inch (3.5 L) metal cake pan with parchment paper; set aside.

←317

← In large bowl, beat butter with brown sugar until fluffy; beat in egg and vanilla. In separate bowl, whisk together rolled oats, flour, baking powder, baking soda and salt; stir in apricots, almonds, cranberries and coconut. Fold into butter mixture. Spread in prepared pan.

← Bake in centre of 350°F (180°C) oven for 30 minutes. Let cool in pan on rack for 10 minutes. Cut into bars. *Make-ahead: Let cool; store in airtight container for up to 1 week.*

PER BAR: about 319 cal, 5 g pro, 15 g total fat (8 g sat. fat), 43 g carb, 3 g fibre, 48 mg chol, 237 mg sodium. % RDI: 4% calcium, 14% iron, 14% vit A, 2% vit C, 10% folate.

TOP 10 MOST REQUES

RECIPES

← 321

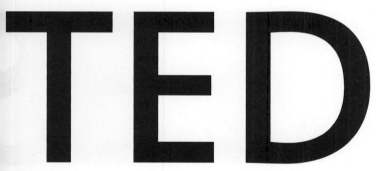

TED

POOL PARTY CAKE

324 →

Last one into the pool gains new meaning when birthday party guests get a look at this cake. Bulk food stores are a good place to find the candies that make this cake so playful.

Makes 16 to 20 servings

1	pkg (85 g) blue jelly powder	1
	White Butter Cake (recipe, opposite)	
2 cups	Basic Butter Icing (recipe, opposite)	500 mL
44	multicoloured cream-filled wafers	44
1	each piece (7 inch/18 cm) red and green shoestring licorice	1
	Pink chocolate rounds, multicoloured sprinkles and chocolate finger cookies	
	Doughnut-shaped jelly candies	
	Gum balls	

↢ Cover bottom and sides of 13- x 9-inch (3.5 L) metal cake pan with plastic wrap; set aside.

↢ Make jelly according to directions on package but use only ¾ cup (175 mL) cold water; pour into prepared pan. Refrigerate, uncovered, until completely set, about 1 hour.

↢ Meanwhile, cut White Butter Cake into kidney shape; place on cake board. With spoon, hollow out ½ inch (1 cm) from top of cake, leaving ¾-inch (2 cm) thick walls as border. Freeze cake scraps for another use.

↢ With palette knife, spread Basic Butter Icing over sides and border of cake. Trim wafers to 2-inch (5 cm) lengths or to match height of cake. Alternating colours, press wafers onto side of cake for fence, leaving 2-inch (5 cm) space uncovered for ladder.

↢ With spatula, pick up long slabs of blue jelly; arrange in hollowed-out centre of cake, rippling to resemble waves.

↢ Cut red piece of licorice in half; arrange both halves on space on side of cake for ladder railings, pressing ends into cake to secure. Cut green licorice into small pieces for ladder steps; secure in place with icing. At opposite end from ladder, press wafer in place for diving board. Around base of pool, arrange pink chocolate rounds and multicoloured sprinkles for landscape. Arrange chocolate finger cookies for wooden planking.

↢ Just before serving, place toy people in doughnut-shaped candy for swimmers in rafts. Add gum balls for beach balls.

PER EACH OF 20 SERVINGS (without candy garnishes): about 325 cal, 3 g pro, 15 g total fat (8 g sat. fat), 47 g carb, trace fibre, 65 mg chol, 269 mg sodium. % RDI: 4% calcium, 9% iron, 13% vit A, 10% folate.

WHITE BUTTER CAKE

Use this delicious and reliable recipe as a foundation for all kinds of special-occasion cakes: anniversaries, showers, graduations and more.

Makes 16 to 20 servings

4	eggs	4
1⅓ cups	milk	325 mL
1 tbsp	vanilla	15 mL
4 cups	sifted cake-and-pastry flour	1 L
2 cups	granulated sugar	500 mL
5 tsp	baking powder	25 mL
1 tbsp	grated orange rind	15 mL
1 tsp	salt	5 mL
1 cup	butter, softened	250 mL

← Grease bottom and sides of 13- x 9-inch (3.5 L) metal cake pan. Line bottom with parchment or waxed paper. Set aside.

← In bowl, whisk together eggs, ⅓ cup (75 mL) of the milk and vanilla; set aside. In large bowl, stir together flour, sugar, baking powder, orange rind and salt; beat in butter and remaining milk at medium speed until fluffy, about 2 minutes. Beat in egg mixture in 3 additions, beating well and scraping down side of bowl after each. Scrape into prepared pan, smoothing top.

← 325

← Bake in centre of 350°F (180°C) oven until golden, cake springs back when lightly touched and tester inserted in centre comes out clean, 40 to 45 minutes. Let cool in pan on rack for 20 minutes.

← Run knife around edge of cake; invert onto baking sheet and peel off paper. Reinvert cake onto rack; let cool. *Make-ahead: Wrap in plastic wrap and store for up to 24 hours. Or overwrap and freeze in rigid airtight container for up to 2 weeks.*

PER EACH OF 20 SERVINGS: about 262 cal, 4 g pro, 11 g total fat (6 g sat. fat), 38 g carb, trace fibre, 67 mg chol, 294 mg sodium. % RDI: 5% calcium, 13% iron, 11% vit A, 13% folate.

BASIC BUTTER ICING

Makes about 2 cups (500 mL)

½ cup	butter, softened	125 mL
2½ cups	icing sugar	625 mL
⅓ cup	whipping cream	75 mL

← In bowl, beat butter at medium speed until light. Alternately beat in sugar and cream, making 3 additions of sugar and 2 of cream. *Make-ahead: Cover and refrigerate for up to 3 days; beat again.*

TIP

For easy decoration and presentation, make a base, or cake board, by using an upside-down jelly roll pan or covering strong cardboard with heavy-duty foil.

CINNAMON BUNS

Hot from the oven and fragrant, scrumptious cinnamon buns are an irresistible combination of feathery light dough, gooey caramelized coating, crunchy pecans and lots of cinnamon. We're sure everyone will appreciate the convenience of the overnight rise in the refrigerator.

Makes 15 buns

¼ cup	granulated sugar	50 mL
½ cup	warm water	125 mL
1	pkg active dry yeast	1
½ cup	milk	125 mL
¼ cup	butter	50 mL
1 tsp	salt	5 mL
2	eggs	2
4 cups	all-purpose flour (approx)	1 L
FILLING		
1 cup	butter	250 mL
1½ cups	packed brown sugar	375 mL
1 cup	coarsely chopped pecans	250 mL
1 tbsp	cinnamon	15 mL

↩ Dissolve 1 tsp (5 mL) of the sugar in warm water. Sprinkle in yeast; let stand until frothy, about 10 minutes.

↩ Meanwhile, in small saucepan, heat together milk, remaining sugar, butter and salt until butter is melted; let cool to lukewarm.

↩ In large bowl, beat eggs; blend in milk mixture and yeast mixture. With mixer, gradually beat in 1½ cups (375 mL) of the flour until smooth, about 2 minutes. With wooden spoon, stir in enough of the remaining flour to make soft slightly sticky dough.

↩ Turn out onto floured surface; knead until smooth and elastic, about 10 minutes, dusting with enough of the remaining flour to prevent sticking. Place in greased bowl, turning to grease all over. Cover with plastic wrap (or greased waxed paper and tea towel); let rise in warm draft-free place until doubled in bulk and impression remains when fingertips are pressed into dough, 1 to 1½ hours (or in refrigerator for 8 hours). Punch down dough.

↩ Grease 13- x 9-inch (3 L) glass baking dish; set aside.

↩ **FILLING:** In saucepan, melt ¾ cup (175 mL) of the butter with ¾ cup (175 mL) of the sugar over medium heat; whisk until smooth. Pour into prepared dish. Sprinkle with half of the pecans. Melt remaining butter. Combine remaining sugar, pecans and cinnamon. Set aside.

↩ On lightly floured surface, roll out dough to 18- x 14-inch (45 x 35 cm) rectangle. Brush with all but 2 tbsp (25 mL) of the melted butter, leaving ½-inch (1 cm) border uncovered. Sprinkle with sugar mixture. Starting at long side, roll up tightly. Brush with remaining butter. With serrated knife cut into 15 pieces; place, cut side down, in dish. Cover and let rise until doubled in bulk, about 1 hour.

↩ Bake in centre of 375°F (190°C) oven until crusts are golden and tops sound hollow when tapped, 25 to 30 minutes. Let stand in pan for 3 minutes. Invert onto serving platter, scraping off any remaining filling in pan to drizzle over buns.

PER BUN: about 423 cal, 6 g pro, 22 g total fat (10 g sat. fat), 52 g carb, 2 g fibre, 74 mg chol, 331 mg sodium. % RDI: 5% calcium, 18% iron, 16% vit A, 27% folate.

STRAWBERRY SHORTCAKE

When you bite into a perfect red strawberry and meet its gush of sweetness, it's easy to understand why this berry is Canada's No. 1 most popular fruit. Match them up with cake and whipped cream and you have a dessert worthy of celebration.

Makes 12 servings

¼ cup	milk	50 mL
2 tbsp	butter	25 mL
1 tsp	grated orange rind	5 mL
¾ cup	sifted cake-and-pastry flour	175 mL
1 tsp	baking powder	5 mL
¼ tsp	salt	1 mL
5	eggs	5
¾ cup	granulated sugar	175 mL
FILLING		
1½ cups	whipping cream	375 mL
2 tbsp	granulated sugar	25 mL
1 tsp	vanilla	5 mL
4 cups	sliced strawberries	1 L
GARNISH		
1 tsp	icing sugar	5 mL
5	whole strawberries	5

← Line 15- x 11-inch (40 x 25 cm) rimmed baking sheet with parchment paper; set aside.

← In saucepan, heat milk with butter over medium heat until butter is melted; stir in orange rind. Set aside and keep warm.

← In bowl, whisk together flour, baking powder and salt; set aside.

← Separate 3 of the eggs, reserving yolks in large bowl. In another bowl, beat egg whites until foamy; beat in ¼ cup (50 mL) of the sugar, 1 tbsp (15 mL) at a time, until soft peaks form.

← Add remaining eggs and sugar to yolks; beat until pale and thick enough that batter leaves ribbons on surface for 3 seconds when beaters are lifted, about 5 minutes. Fold in whites. Sift dry ingredients over top; fold in until combined. Make well in centre; pour in milk mixture and fold in.

← Spread in prepared pan. Bake in centre of 350°F (180°C) oven until golden and cake springs back when lightly touched, about 12 minutes. Let cool in pan on rack.

← FILLING: In bowl, whip cream with sugar and vanilla. Cut cake crosswise into thirds; transfer one of the thirds to flat serving plate or tray. Spread with half of the whipped cream, then half of the strawberries. Top with second cake layer; spread with remaining cream, then berries. Top with remaining cake layer. Cover and refrigerate for 1 hour.

← GARNISH: Using fine sieve, dust icing sugar evenly over top by tapping sieve gently. Garnish with whole berries.

PER SERVING: about 248 cal, 4 g pro, 15 g total fat (8 g sat. fat), 26 g carb, 1 g fibre, 133 mg chol, 129 mg sodium. % RDI: 5% calcium, 7% iron, 18% vit A, 53% vit C, 9% folate.

TIP

Rimmed baking sheets are also known as jelly roll pans.

WHITE CHOCOLATE CHEESECAKE WITH FRUIT AND RASPBERRY COULIS

330 →

Just a small slice of this dense cheesecake is divine, but be lavish with the fruit that tops and spills over each serving.

Makes 16 servings

60	vanilla wafers (about 6 oz/175 g)	60
½ cup	butter, melted	125 mL
8 oz	white chocolate, coarsely chopped	250 g
1 cup	10% cream	250 mL
3	pkg (each 8 oz/250 g) cream cheese, softened	3
¼ cup	granulated sugar	50 mL
4	eggs	4
2 tsp	vanilla	10 mL
¾ cup	Raspberry Coulis (recipe, opposite)	175 mL
4 cups	sliced fresh fruit and berries	1 L

← Grease bottom and side of 9-inch (2.5 L) springform pan; line side with parchment paper. Set on large wide piece of heavy-duty foil; press foil against side of pan.

← In food processor, grind vanilla wafers to fine crumbs; add butter and blend until evenly moistened. Press onto bottom and ½ inch (1 cm) up side of prepared pan. Bake in centre of 350°F (180°C) oven until golden brown at edge, about 15 minutes. Let cool on rack.

← Meanwhile, in bowl over saucepan of hot (not boiling) water, melt white chocolate with cream; gently stir until smooth. Let cool to room temperature.

← In separate bowl, beat cream cheese with sugar until fluffy; beat in eggs, 1 at a time, beating well after each addition. Stir in white chocolate mixture and vanilla. Pour into cooled crust.

← Set pan in larger pan; pour in enough hot water to come 1 inch (2.5 cm) up sides. Bake in centre of 325°F (160°C) oven until centre is just set and edge is slightly puffed, about 1 hour and 15 minutes. Most cheesecakes are still slightly jiggly when done, but because of the white chocolate, this one is quite firm and is set. If jiggly, it is still underdone. Remove from water bath and place on rack; remove foil and let cool completely. *Make-ahead: Cover and refrigerate for up to 2 days.*

← Pool Raspberry Coulis on dessert plates; place slice of cheesecake on coulis. Top with fruit.

PER SERVING: about 427 cal, 7 g pro, 31 g total fat (18 g sat. fat), 31 g carb, 1 g fibre, 130 mg chol, 267 mg sodium. % RDI: 9% calcium, 9% iron, 28% vit A, 28% vit C, 14% folate.

RASPBERRY COULIS

← 331

Makes 1 cup (250 mL)

2 cups	unsweetened raspberries (fresh or thawed)	500 mL
1 tbsp	lemon juice	15 mL
3 tbsp	granulated sugar	50 mL

← In blender or food processor, purée raspberries with lemon juice until smooth. Strain through fine sieve into bowl; stir in sugar. *Make-ahead: Cover and refrigerate for up to 3 days.*

PER 1 TBSP (15 mL): about 13 cal, trace pro, 0 g total fat (0 g sat. fat), 3 g carb, 0 g fibre, 0 mg chol, 0 mg sodium. % RDI: 1% iron, 5% vit C, 1% folate.

TIP

You can also use 1¾ cups (425 mL) graham cracker crumbs instead of the vanilla wafers.

PEPPY SALSA

As sure as August rolls around, the calls and e-mails come to the Test Kitchen asking for this recipe. We all find this salsa easy to make and just as delicious as old-time chili sauce and ketchup, plus it uses a lot less sugar.

Makes 11 cups (2.75 L)

8 oz	jalapeño peppers	250 g
8 cups	coarsely chopped peeled tomatoes	2 L
3 cups	chopped seeded Cubanelle, Anaheim or sweet banana peppers	750 mL
2 cups	chopped onions	500 mL
2 cups	cider vinegar	500 mL
1 cup	each chopped sweet red and yellow peppers	250 mL
4	cloves garlic, minced	4
1	can (5½ oz/156 mL) tomato paste	1
2 tbsp	granulated sugar	25 mL
1 tbsp	salt	15 mL
2 tsp	paprika	10 mL
1 tsp	dried oregano	5 mL
¼ cup	chopped fresh coriander	50 mL

↩ 333

↩ Wearing rubber gloves, seed, core and finely chop jalapeño peppers to make 1 cup (250 mL).

↩ In large heavy nonaluminum pot, combine jalapeños, tomatoes, Cubanelle peppers, onions, vinegar, red and yellow peppers, garlic, tomato paste, sugar, salt, paprika and oregano; bring to boil, stirring often. Reduce heat to medium-low; simmer, stirring often, until thickened enough that 1 tbsp (15 mL) dropped onto plate flows slowly in 1 stream when plate is tilted, about 1 hour.

↩ Add coriander; simmer, stirring occasionally, for 5 minutes.

↩ Using funnel and ladle, fill hot sterilized 2-cup (500 mL) jars, leaving ½-inch (1 cm) headspace. If necessary, wipe rims with damp paper towels. Cover with prepared lids; screw on bands fingertip tight.

↩ Process in boiling water canner for 20 minutes. Transfer jars to rack; let cool, undisturbed, for 24 hours. Check for seal, ensuring that lids curve downward. If not, refrigerate and use within 3 weeks. Store in cool, dry, dark place. Refrigerate after opening.

PER 1 TBSP (15 mL): about 6 cal, trace pro, 0 g total fat (0 g sat. fat), 1 g carb, trace fibre, 0 mg chol, 41 mg sodium. % RDI: 1% iron, 2% vit A, 17% vit C, 1% folate.

TIP

For a fiery-hot salsa, use small Scotch bonnet peppers or long thin red chili peppers. For a milder version, substitute sweet peppers for the jalapeños.

CRAB CAKES WITH CHIPOTLE MAYONNAISE

When a platter of crab cakes starts to circulate at a party, just watch the crowd form and the crisp patties disappear. Try them with all three different flavourings — chipotle, Cajun and curried as in the photograph.

Makes 16 pieces

1	pkg (7 oz/200 g) frozen crabmeat, thawed	1
⅓ cup	finely diced sweet red pepper	75 mL
¼ cup	finely diced sweet green pepper	50 mL
¼ cup	chopped green onions	50 mL
1	egg, beaten	1
1¼ cups	dry bread crumbs	300 mL
2 tbsp	vegetable oil	25 mL

CHIPOTLE MAYONNAISE

2	chipotle peppers, finely chopped	2
½ cup	light mayonnaise	125 mL
1 tbsp	adobo sauce	15 mL
Dash	Worcestershire sauce	Dash

← Line rimmed baking sheet with waxed paper; set aside.

← **CHIPOTLE MAYONNAISE:** In small bowl, whisk together chipotle peppers, mayonnaise, adobo sauce and Worcestershire sauce; set aside.

← In sieve set over bowl, pick through crabmeat to remove any cartilage; press firmly to remove liquid. Transfer to large bowl.

← Add red and green peppers, onions, egg, 2 tbsp (25 mL) of the bread crumbs and 3 tbsp (50 mL) of the Chipotle Mayonnaise; stir until combined.

← Form by rounded 1 tbsp (15 mL) into balls; roll in remaining bread crumbs. Place on prepared baking sheet; flatten to 2-inch (5 cm) diameter. *Make-ahead: Cover and refrigerate for up to 24 hours.*

← In nonstick skillet, heat half of the oil over medium-high heat; fry crab cakes, in batches and using enough of the remaining oil as necessary, until golden, about 3 minutes per side. Serve with remaining Chipotle Mayonnaise.

PER PIECE: about 93 cal, 5 g pro, 5 g total fat (trace sat. fat), 8 g carb, trace fibre, 22 mg chol, 214 mg sodium. % RDI: 2% calcium, 6% iron, 3% vit A, 13% vit C, 5% folate.

VARIATIONS

CRAB CAKES WITH CURRIED MANGO CHUTNEY MAYONNAISE

Substitute 1 tbsp (15 mL) mango chutney (pieces finely chopped if necessary) and 1 tsp (5 mL) mild or hot curry paste for the chipotles and adobo sauce.

CRAB CAKES WITH CAJUN MAYONNAISE

Substitute 1 tbsp (15 mL) grainy mustard and ½ tsp (2 mL) Cajun seasoning for the chipotles and adobo sauce.

TIP

Chipotles are smoked jalapeño peppers packed in adobo sauce. If unavailable, use 1 tbsp (15 mL) each ketchup and minced jalapeño for the chipotles and adobo sauce.

HALLOWEEN
SPIDER WEB DIP

336 → This spooky presentation of guacamole, bean dip and salsa will keep hungry pumpkin carvers grinning. We like it with lots of tortilla chips.

Makes 5½ cups (1.375 L)

1 tbsp	vegetable oil	15 mL
1	onion, chopped	1
4	cloves garlic, minced	4
¼ tsp	each salt and pepper	1 mL
1	can (19 oz/540 mL) pinto or white kidney beans, drained and rinsed	1
2	avocados	2
¼ cup	light mayonnaise	50 mL
2 tbsp	lime juice	25 mL
2 cups	salsa	500 mL
½ cup	light sour cream	125 mL
2	black olives, halved and pitted	2

← In skillet, heat oil over medium heat; fry onion, half of the garlic, the salt and pepper until softened, about 5 minutes. Add beans; cook over medium-low heat until hot, about 5 minutes. Using potato masher or fork, mash until almost smooth; let cool.

← Meanwhile, cut each avocado in half and pit; using spoon, scoop flesh into bowl. Mash until smooth; stir in mayonnaise, lime juice and remaining garlic.

← Evenly spread bean mixture in 8-inch (20 cm) pie plate or serving dish. Spread salsa, then avocado mixture evenly over top. *Make-ahead: Place plastic wrap directly on surface; refrigerate for up to 1 hour.*

← Spoon sour cream into plastic bag; cut off tip of 1 corner. Pipe in concentric circles over top. From centre to rim, pull knife through sour cream at even intervals to form web pattern. In centre, place 2 olive halves end to end to form spider body. Cut remaining olive halves into 8 slivers; arrange around body for legs.

PER 1 TBSP (15 mL): about 19 cal, 1 g pro, 1 g total fat (trace sat. fat), 2 g carb, 1 g fibre, 0 mg chol, 44 mg sodium. % RDI: 1% calcium, 1% iron, 1% vit A, 3% vit C, 3% folate.

"PUMPKIN" CHEESE BALL

A classic cheese ball gets all dressed up for Halloween. Surround it with crackers and celery sticks for spreading.

← 337

Makes 3 cups (750 mL)

1	pkg (250 g) cream cheese, softened	1
2 cups	shredded orange old Cheddar cheese	500 mL
2 tbsp	each diced onion, carrot and celery	25 mL
1 tbsp	minced fresh parsley	15 mL
1 tsp	prepared horseradish	5 mL
1	broccoli stem (3 inches/ 8 cm long), peeled	1

← In large bowl, beat cream cheese until smooth; stir in Cheddar cheese, onion, carrot, celery, parsley and horseradish. Form into ball; wrap in plastic wrap. Refrigerate until firm, about 1 hour. *Make-ahead: Refrigerate for up to 3 days.*

← Unwrap ball and flatten slightly; insert broccoli stem at top to resemble pumpkin stem. Using handle of wooden spoon, draw vertical ridges at even intervals in side to resemble pumpkin.

PER 1 TBSP (15 mL): about 38 cal, 2 g pro, 3 g total fat (2 g sat. fat), trace carb, trace fibre, 11 mg chol, 45 mg sodium. % RDI: 4% calcium, 1% iron, 5% vit A, 1% folate.

PORK TENDERLOIN WITH MUSHROOM STUFFING AND PAN-SEARED ONION AND APPLES

338 →

This incredibly tender, lean, moist cut of pork has no waste and lends itself perfectly to the delights of a herbed mushroom stuffing. Serve it hot from the oven or make it ahead to serve cold, omitting the onion and apples.

Makes 8 to 10 servings

3	boneless pork tenderloins (each 12 oz/375 g)	3
¼ cup	Dijon mustard	50 mL
1	apple (unpeeled), thinly sliced	1
¼ tsp	each salt and pepper	1 mL
6	fresh thyme sprigs	6
	Pan-Seared Onion and Apples (recipe, opposite)	

STUFFING

2 tbsp	each butter and vegetable oil	25 mL
4 cups	finely diced mushrooms (about 14 oz/400 g)	1 L
¾ cup	finely chopped onions or shallots	175 mL
1	apple (unpeeled), diced	1
1	carrot, finely chopped	1
2 cups	coarse fresh bread crumbs	500 mL
⅓ cup	chopped fresh parsley	75 mL
1 tbsp	chopped fresh thyme (or ½ tsp/2 mL dried)	15 mL
¼ tsp	crumbled dried sage	1 mL
¼ tsp	each salt and pepper	1 mL

STUFFING: In large skillet, heat butter with oil over medium-high heat; fry mushrooms and onions, stirring occasionally, until liquid is evaporated, about 8 minutes. Add apple and carrot; sauté for 1 minute. Remove from heat. Add bread crumbs, parsley, thyme, sage, salt and pepper; combine well. Set aside.

Cut each tenderloin lengthwise halfway through; open like book. Place between plastic wrap or waxed paper; using meat pounder or rolling pin, pound to generous ¼-inch (5 mm) thickness.

Cut about 7 pieces of kitchen string into 15-inch (38 cm) lengths; arrange crosswise about 1½ inches (4 cm) apart in lightly greased roasting pan. Place 1 piece of meat on strings. With hands, press half of the stuffing over meat to cover surface. Top with second piece of meat, placing wide end over thin end of first piece; tuck thin ends under and press firmly in place. Top with remaining stuffing and meat. Tie strings around roast, trimming any excess.

Spread mustard all over roast. Arrange apple slices in lengthwise row on top; sprinkle with salt and pepper. Arrange thyme sprigs over top. Place in 400°F (200°C) oven; reduce heat to 350°F (180°C) and roast until meat thermometer registers 160°F (70°C), 1¼ to 1¾ hours. Transfer to cutting board; tent with foil. Let stand for 10 minutes. *Make-ahead: Let cool, cover and refrigerate for up to 24 hours.*

Slice roast and arrange on platter; surround with Pan-Seared Onion and Apples.

PER EACH OF 10 SERVINGS (including onion and apples): about 319 cal, 27 g pro, 13 g total fat (3 g sat. fat), 26 g carb, 4 g fibre, 66 mg chol, 318 mg sodium. % RDI: 4% calcium, 18% iron, 21% vit A, 13% vit C, 11% folate.

PAN-SEARED ONION AND APPLES

Makes 8 to 10 servings

3	large apples	3
1	large red onion	1
3 tbsp	vegetable oil (approx)	**50 mL**

← Cut uncored apples crosswise into scant ½-inch (1 cm) thick slices. Discard ends. Repeat with onion.

← In large skillet, heat half of the oil over medium-high heat; sear apples and onion until browned, 1 to 2 minutes per side and adding more oil if necessary.

PER EACH OF 10 SERVINGS: about 87 cal, 1 g pro, 4 g total fat (trace sat. fat), 13 g carb, 2 g fibre, 0 mg chol, 1 mg sodium. % RDI: 1% calcium, 1% iron, 7% vit C, 3% folate.

KOREAN HOT WINGS WITH GARLICKY SOY DIPPING SAUCE

Everybody loves wings, and these fabulous ones, which rate medium-hot on the pub scale, are so much better than any you can buy or order. For a timid version, omit the cayenne pepper in the wings and the hot pepper flakes in the dipping sauce.

Makes 25 to 30 pieces

2 tbsp	soy sauce	25 mL
1 tbsp	sesame seeds	15 mL
1 tbsp	grated gingerroot	15 mL
1 tbsp	sesame oil	15 mL
1½ tsp	granulated sugar	7 mL
½ tsp	pepper	2 mL
Pinch	cayenne pepper	Pinch
2	cloves garlic, minced	2
2 lb	chicken wings, tips removed	1 kg
	Garlicky Soy Dipping Sauce (recipe, this page)	

← In large bowl, mix together soy sauce, sesame seeds, ginger, sesame oil, sugar, pepper, cayenne pepper and garlic. Add chicken wings; toss to coat well. Cover and marinate in refrigerator for 2 hours. *Make-ahead: Refrigerate for up to 24 hours.*

← Arrange wings on rack on foil-lined rimmed baking sheet. Bake in 400°F (200°C) oven for 20 minutes; turn and bake until juices run clear when chicken is pierced, about 15 minutes.

← Broil wings, turning once, until crisp and browned, 1 to 2 minutes per side. Serve with Garlicky Soy Dipping Sauce.

PER EACH OF 30 PIECES: about 43 cal, 3 g pro, 3 g total fat (1 g sat. fat), 1 g carb, 0 g fibre, 9 mg chol, 125 mg sodium. % RDI: 1% iron, 1% vit A.

GARLICKY SOY DIPPING SAUCE

Makes about ¼ cup (50 mL)

2 tbsp	minced green onions	25 mL
4 tsp	soy sauce	20 mL
1 tbsp	rice vinegar	15 mL
½ tsp	sesame oil	2 mL
2	cloves garlic, minced	2
½ tsp	granulated sugar	2 mL
¼ tsp	hot pepper flakes	1 mL

← In bowl, mix together onions, soy sauce, vinegar, sesame oil, garlic, sugar and hot pepper flakes.

PER 1 TSP (5 mL): about 5 cal, trace pro, trace total fat (0 g sat. fat), 1 g carb, 0 g fibre, 0 mg chol, 115 mg sodium. % RDI: 1% iron.

CHICKEN ENCHILADAS

This rolled-tortilla casserole comes together deliciously with ingredients you can find in the supermarket.

Makes 8 servings

8	large flour tortillas	8
TOMATO SAUCE		
1 tbsp	vegetable oil	15 mL
1	onion, minced	1
2	cloves garlic, minced	2
2 tbsp	chili powder	25 mL
1 tsp	each ground coriander and dried oregano	5 mL
½ tsp	each ground cumin and salt	2 mL
¼ tsp	pepper	1 mL
1	can (28 oz/796 mL) ground tomatoes	1
CHICKEN FILLING		
2 lb	boneless skinless chicken thighs	1 kg
1 tbsp	vegetable oil	15 mL
1	sweet yellow or red pepper, sliced	1
1	jalapeño pepper, seeded and minced	1
¼ tsp	each salt and pepper	1 mL
2 cups	shredded Monterey Jack cheese	500 mL
¼ cup	chopped fresh coriander	50 mL

← **TOMATO SAUCE:** In large saucepan, heat oil over medium heat; fry onion, garlic, chili powder, coriander, oregano, cumin, salt and pepper, stirring occasionally, until softened, 5 minutes.

← Add tomatoes and bring to boil; reduce heat and simmer until spoon scraped across bottom of pan leaves gap that fills in slowly, about 20 minutes.

← **CHICKEN FILLING:** Trim fat from chicken; cut crosswise into ¼-inch (5 mm) thick slices. In large skillet, heat oil over medium-high heat; brown chicken, in batches. Transfer to bowl.

← Drain fat from pan. Add yellow and jalapeño peppers, salt and pepper; fry over medium heat, stirring, until tender-crisp, about 3 minutes. Add to chicken; let cool. Stir in 1 cup (250 mL) of the Monterey Jack cheese and 2 tbsp (25 mL) of the coriander.

← Spread 1 cup (250 mL) of the tomato sauce in 13- x 9- inch (3 L) glass baking dish. Spoon heaping ½ cup (125 mL) of the filling down centre of each tortilla; roll up tightly and place, seam side down, in dish. *Make-ahead: Let enchiladas and remaining tomato sauce cool separately for 30 minutes; chill in refrigerator. Cover and refrigerate for up to 24 hours. Or wrap in heavy-duty foil and freeze for up to 2 weeks; thaw in refrigerator for 24 hours. Add 10 minutes to covered baking time.*

← Spoon remaining tomato sauce over enchiladas. Cover with foil; bake in 375°F (190°C) oven for 30 minutes. Sprinkle with remaining cheese; bake, uncovered, until tip of knife inserted in centre of enchilada for 5 seconds comes out hot, about 10 minutes. Sprinkle with remaining coriander.

PER SERVING: about 515 cal, 36 g pro, 22 g total fat (8 g sat. fat), 43 g carb, 5 g fibre, 119 mg chol, 891 mg sodium. % RDI: 27% calcium, 37% iron, 24% vit A, 65% vit C, 45% folate.

CHAPTER 10
TEST KITCHE FAVOU ITES

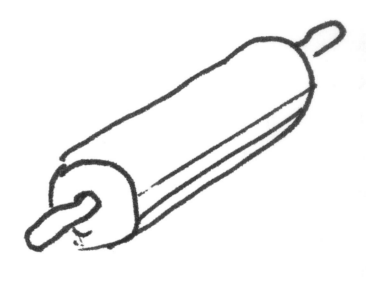

SMOKED SALMON AND RADISH DIP

Scoop up this tasty and crunchy firm dip with crackers and crudités. It doesn't matter who's coming to a Test Kitchen party, this is the dip we like to serve. It just goes to show how far you can go with a small package of smoked salmon.

← 351

Makes about 2 cups (500 mL)

¾ cup	sour cream	175 mL
½ cup	low-fat pressed cottage cheese	125 mL
½ cup	cream cheese, softened	125 mL
Pinch	each salt and pepper	Pinch
4 oz	smoked salmon, finely chopped	125 g
½ cup	finely chopped red radishes	125 mL
⅓ cup	finely chopped red onion	75 mL
2 tbsp	chopped fresh chives or green part of green onion	25 mL

← In large bowl, beat together sour cream, cottage cheese, cream cheese, salt and pepper. Stir in salmon, radishes, onion and chives. Transfer to serving bowl. *Make-ahead: Cover and refrigerate for up to 8 hours.*

PER 1 TBSP (15 mL): about 30 cal, 2 g pro, 2 g total fat (1 g sat. fat), 1 g carb, trace fibre, 7 mg chol, 42 mg sodium. % RDI: 1% calcium, 1% iron, 2% vit A, 2% vit C, 1% folate.

TIP

Smoked salmon varies in its degree of saltiness. You can omit the salt and taste for seasoning just before serving, if desired.

SWISS PORK
AND MUSHROOMS

352 → It only takes 20 minutes to make these tender strips of pork in a party-style creamy mushroom sauce.

Makes 4 servings

1 lb	pork loin centre chops boneless	**500 g**
1 tbsp	extra-virgin olive oil	**15 mL**
Half	onion, diced	**Half**
2 cups	sliced mushrooms	**500 mL**
2	cloves garlic, minced	**2**
¼ tsp	salt	**1 mL**
Pinch	pepper	**Pinch**
½ cup	light sour cream	**125 mL**
¼ cup	chicken stock	**50 mL**
1 tsp	lemon juice	**5 mL**
1 tbsp	chopped fresh parsley	**15 mL**

← Cut pork crosswise into thin strips. In large nonstick skillet, heat oil over medium-high heat; stir-fry pork, in batches, until browned but still slightly pink inside, 2 to 3 minutes. With slotted spoon, transfer to plate.

← Add onion, mushrooms, garlic, salt and pepper to pan; fry over medium heat, stirring occasionally, until no liquid remains, about 10 minutes.

← Return pork to pan. Stir in sour cream and stock; cook, without boiling, until hot, about 1 minute. Stir in lemon juice. Sprinkle with parsley.

PER SERVING: about 246 cal, 28 g pro, 12 g total fat (4 g sat. fat), 6 g carb, 1 g fibre, 70 mg chol, 291 mg sodium. % RDI: 8% calcium, 11% iron, 2% vit A, 7% vit C, 5% folate.

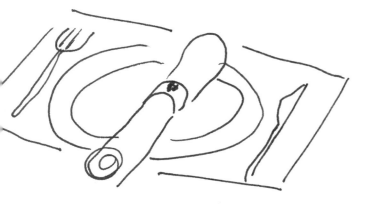

DILLED CARROTS

Instead of the four carrots, you can also use one bag (340 g) baby carrots.

← 353

Makes 4 servings

4	carrots, sliced	4
1 tbsp	butter	15 mL
½ tsp	dried dillweed	2 mL

← In saucepan of boiling salted water, cover and cook carrots until tender-crisp, about 5 minutes; drain. (Or in microwaveable dish, cover and microwave carrots and ¼ cup/50 mL water at high for 5 to 7 minutes; drain.)

← Toss with butter and dillweed.

PER SERVING: about 59 cal, 1 g pro, 3 g total fat (2 g sat. fat), 8 g carb, 2 g fibre, 9 mg chol, 78 mg sodium. % RDI: 2% calcium, 4% iron, 185% vit A, 3% vit C, 5% folate.

SMOKY PAPRIKA SHRIMP

There are sweet and hot varieties of paprika as well as the irresistible Spanish smoked version *(pimentón de la Vera)*. It's becoming available in Canada and complements big juicy shrimp like no other. However, substitute sweet paprika if smoked is unavailable.

Makes 8 servings

2 tbsp	extra-virgin olive oil	25 mL
6	cloves garlic, minced	6
1 lb	large raw shrimp, peeled and deveined	500 g
1 tbsp	smoked paprika	15 mL
⅓ cup	white wine	75 mL
2 tsp	tomato paste	10 mL
¼ tsp	salt	1 mL
2 tbsp	chopped fresh parsley or coriander	25 mL

← In large skillet, heat oil over medium heat; fry garlic until softened but not browned, about 2 minutes. Add shrimp and paprika; fry, stirring, until shrimp are coated and beginning to turn pink, about 2 minutes.

← Stir in wine, tomato paste and salt; cook over high heat, stirring, until shrimp are pink and almost all liquid is evaporated, about 2 minutes. Sprinkle with parsley.

← 355

PER SERVING: about 88 cal, 9 g pro, 4 g total fat (1 g sat. fat), 2 g carb, trace fibre, 55 mg chol, 137 mg sodium. % RDI: 2% calcium, 9% iron, 8% vit A, 5% vit C, 2% folate.

TIP

You can freeze leftover tomato paste in convenient amounts for recipes. Spoon 1 tbsp (15 mL) portions in line along piece of plastic wrap; fold wrap over to enclose and twist between "beads." Clean tomato paste can and store beads inside for easy identification. Snip off beads as needed. Or use Italian tomato paste in a tube.

SCALLOPED POTATOES

While some old-fashioned dishes don't live up to their reputation, this golden crusty-topped layered potato favourite certainly does — in spades.

Makes 6 servings

6	Yukon Gold potatoes (about 2 lb/1 kg)	6
1	small onion, sliced	1
SAUCE		
¼ cup	butter	50 mL
¼ cup	all-purpose flour	50 mL
1 tsp	salt	5 mL
½ tsp	pepper	2 mL
½ tsp	dried thyme or marjoram	2 mL
2½ cups	milk	625 mL

← 357

← **SAUCE:** In saucepan, melt butter over medium heat. Add flour, salt, pepper and thyme; cook, stirring, for 1 minute. Gradually whisk in milk; cook, whisking constantly, until boiling and thickened, 5 to 8 minutes. Set aside.

← Peel and thinly slice potatoes. Layer one-third in greased 8-inch (2 L) square glass baking dish or casserole; spread half of the onions over top. Repeat layers. Arrange remaining potatoes over top. Pour sauce over top, using tip of knife to ease sauce between layers.

← Cover and bake in 350°F (180°C) oven for 1 hour. Uncover and bake until lightly browned and potatoes are tender, about 30 minutes longer. Let stand for 5 minutes before serving.

PER SERVING: about 256 cal, 6 g pro, 10 g total fat (5 g sat. fat), 36 g carb, 2 g fibre, 28 mg chol, 518 mg sodium. % RDI: 13% calcium, 6% iron, 12% vit A, 18% vit C, 10% folate.

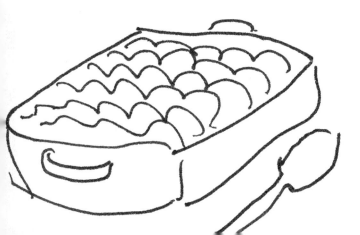

ROASTED DOUBLE-SALMON FILLET WITH SPINACH MUSHROOM FILLING

For this impressive company dish, it's important to buy two matching pieces of centre-cut salmon. Ask the fishmonger to remove any flat flap of belly before weighing. Of course, if he removes the skin, too, it saves you a step.

Makes 8 servings

2	centre-cut salmon fillets, 6 inches (15 cm) long x 1 inch (2.5 cm) thick (2 lb/1 kg total)	2
¼ cup	herbed cream cheese	50 mL
2 tbsp	butter, softened	25 mL
¼ tsp	each salt and pepper	1 mL
SPINACH MUSHROOM FILLING		
2½ cups	oyster mushrooms (4 oz/125 g) or button mushrooms (6 oz/175 g)	625 mL
2 tsp	vegetable oil	10 mL
1 tbsp	balsamic vinegar	15 mL
1	pkg (6 oz/175 g) fresh baby spinach	1
¼ tsp	each salt and pepper	1 mL

← **SPINACH MUSHROOM FILLING:** Slice mushrooms. In large skillet, heat oil over medium heat; fry mushrooms, stirring occasionally, until golden and no liquid remains, about 10 minutes. Sprinkle with vinegar; toss to coat. Transfer to bowl.

← Meanwhile, rinse spinach; shake off excess water. In large saucepan, cover and cook spinach over medium heat, with just the water clinging to leaves and stirring once, until wilted, about 3 minutes. Transfer to sieve; press out moisture. Chop and add to mushroom mixture along with salt and pepper. *Make-ahead: Cover and refrigerate for up to 24 hours.*

← To remove skin, place each salmon fillet, skin side down, on cutting board. At one end, cut between flesh and skin just enough to grip skin. Holding skin with paper towel and knife flat but without moving, pull skin back and forth to remove. Discard skin.

← In small bowl, mash cream cheese to soften; spread over skinned side of fillets. Spread filling over cream cheese on 1 of the fillets, leaving ½-inch (1 cm) border. Top with remaining fillet, cheese side down. Tie together at 1-inch (2.5 cm) intervals. Place on greased rimmed baking sheet. Spread butter over top; sprinkle with salt and pepper. *Make-ahead: Cover and refrigerate for up to 8 hours.*

← Roast in 400°F (200°C) oven until golden and fish flakes easily when tested, about 40 minutes. Transfer to cutting board; let stand for 5 minutes. Using serrated knife and sawing motion, cut crosswise into 1-inch (2.5 cm) thick portions.

PER SERVING: about 308 cal, 25 g pro, 21 g total fat (7 g sat. fat), 3 g carb, 1 g fibre, 88 mg chol, 365 mg sodium. % RDI: 6% calcium, 11% iron, 29% vit A, 12% vit C, 36% folate.

VARIATION

ROASTED DOUBLE-SALMON FILLET WITH DILLED CRAB AND RED PEPPER FILLING

Omit filling. Combine 7 oz (200 g) frozen crabmeat, thawed and pressed to remove moisture; ¼ cup (50 mL) each finely chopped green onion, chopped roasted sweet red pepper and mayonnaise; 2 tbsp (25 mL) chopped fresh dill ; and ¼ tsp (1 mL) each salt and pepper.

LACY GOLDEN LATKES

360 →

Latkes are the crisp potato pancakes that are so anticipated at the Jewish festival of Hanukkah. The Test Kitchen finds these lacy, golden rounds so irresistible that we grate up pounds of potatoes and fry up enough for a great latke party every holiday season. We serve them to the staff with big bowls of sour cream and Chunky Honey Applesauce or Chunky Cran-Apple Sauce (recipes, opposite).

Makes about 22 latkes or 4 to 6 servings

5	baking potatoes (about 2½ lb/1.25 kg)	5
2	small onions, quartered	2
3	eggs	3
3 tbsp	all-purpose flour (or ¼ cup/50 mL matzo meal)	50 mL
¾ tsp	salt	4 mL
¼ tsp	pepper	1 mL
	Vegetable oil for cooking	

← Peel potatoes. By hand or in food processor using shredder blade, alternately shred onion quarters and potatoes. Transfer to colander; squeeze out as much moisture as possible and discard liquid. Transfer to large bowl.

← Mix eggs, flour, salt and pepper into potato mixture; let stand for 5 minutes. Pour out any liquid.

← In large skillet, heat ¼ inch (5 mm) oil over high heat until hot but not smoking. Add ¼ cup (50 mL) mixture per latke, leaving about 1 inch (2.5 cm) space between each. Flatten slightly with back of spoon. Fry until browned and crisp around edges, reducing heat if necessary to prevent burning, about 3 minutes.

← With slotted spatula, turn and fry until crisp and golden brown, 2 to 3 minutes. Transfer to paper towels; drain well. Repeat with remaining mixture, removing any cooked bits from pan and heating more oil as necessary. *Make-ahead: Cover and refrigerate for up to 8 hours; recrisp on rimmed baking sheets in 450°F/230°C oven for about 5 minutes.*

PER LATKE: about 108 cal, 2 g pro, 7 g total fat (1 g sat. fat), 9 g carb, 1 g fibre, 25 mg chol, 89 mg sodium. % RDI: 1% calcium, 2% iron, 1% vit A, 5% vit C, 4% folate.

TIP

Shredding the potatoes alternately with the onions prevents them from discolouring.

CHUNKY HONEY APPLESAUCE

This has more texture and flavour and is a bit less sweet than the store-bought variety.

← 361

Makes about 2½ cups (625 mL)

6	apples (such as Northern Spy or Golden Delicious)	6
⅓ cup	apple juice	75 mL
2 tbsp	lemon juice	25 mL
2 tbsp	liquid honey	25 mL
Pinch	cinnamon	Pinch

← Peel, core and cube apples. In large saucepan, bring apples, apple juice, lemon juice, honey and cinnamon to boil; reduce heat to low and simmer, stirring often, until tender, about 30 minutes.
← With potato masher, mash until starting to break up but still chunky.

PER ¼ CUP (50 mL): about 68 cal, trace pro, trace total fat (0 g sat. fat), 18 g carb, 2 g fibre, 0 mg chol 1 mg sodium. % RDI: 1% iron, 10% vit C.

VARIATION

CHUNKY CRAN-APPLE SAUCE

Replace 2 of the apples with 1½ cups (375 mL) fresh or frozen cranberries. Increase honey to ¼ cup (50 mL).

WILD BLUEBERRY BUNDT CAKE

Around Oxford, N.S., the rolling hills are blue with berries and it's a feast of fresh wild blueberries, preserves and desserts. These are the inspiration for this handsome cake we like to serve with ice cream. To use one of the decorative Bundt pans, bake the cake in 325°F (160°C) oven for 55 to 65 minutes.

Makes 12 servings

1 cup	butter, softened	250 mL
1½ cups	granulated sugar	375 mL
4	eggs, separated	4
2 tbsp	coarsely grated orange rind	25 mL
3 cups	all-purpose flour	750 mL
1 tbsp	baking powder	15 mL
½ tsp	salt	2 mL
1 cup	orange juice	250 mL
4 cups	fresh blueberries (preferably wild)	1 L
GLAZE		
½ cup	granulated sugar	125 mL
½ cup	orange juice	125 mL

← 363

← Grease 10-inch (3 L) Bundt pan or angel food cake pan; dust with flour. Set aside.

← In large bowl, beat butter with 1 cup (250 mL) of the sugar until fluffy. Beat in egg yolks, 1 at a time; beat in orange rind. In separate bowl and using clean beaters, beat egg whites until soft peaks form. Beat in remaining sugar, 1 tbsp (15 mL) at a time, until firm glossy peaks form. Set aside.

← In third bowl, whisk together flour, baking powder and salt. With wooden spoon, stir into butter mixture alternately with orange juice, making 3 additions of dry ingredients and 2 of juice to make stiff batter. Stir in one-third of the egg whites; fold in remaining egg whites. Fold in 2 cups (500 mL) of the blueberries. Scrape into prepared pan; smooth top and tap pan gently on counter.

← Bake in centre of 350°F (180°C) oven until cake tester inserted in centre comes out clean, 45 to 55 minutes. Transfer to rack; let cool for 20 minutes.

← **GLAZE:** Meanwhile, in small saucepan, bring sugar and orange juice to boil, stirring; boil for 1 minute. Let cool.

← Loosen cake from edges of pan; invert onto rack. Place foil below rack; brush cake with glaze. Let cool. Transfer to flat serving plate; fill centre with remaining blueberries.

PER SERVING: about 444 cal, 6 g pro, 18 g total fat (10 g sat. fat), 68 g carb, 2 g fibre, 110 mg chol, 341 mg sodium. % RDI: 5% calcium, 13% iron, 18% vit A, 23% vit C, 25% folate.

TIP

To dust the inside of a cake pan with flour, scoop a heaping tablespoonful (15 mL) all-purpose flour into the greased pan. Shake pan back and forth to coat bottom, then tilt and rotate pan to cover entire inside. Hold pan upside down and tap out excess flour.

CHOCOLATE RASPBERRY CAKE

This dense chocolate cake layered with seedless raspberry jam is a cinch to cut, and its generous size makes it a real crowd-pleaser for birthdays, showers, anniversaries and any other celebration.

Makes 24 to 32 servings

1½ cups	butter, softened	375 mL
2¼ cups	granulated sugar	550 mL
3	eggs	3
1½ tsp	vanilla	7 mL
3 cups	all-purpose flour	750 mL
¾ cup	cocoa powder	175 mL
1½ tsp	each baking powder and baking soda	7 mL
½ tsp	salt	2 mL
2¼ cups	buttermilk	550 mL
CHOCOLATE GLAZE		
8 oz	bittersweet or semisweet chocolate, chopped	250 g
¼ cup	butter	50 mL
2 tbsp	corn syrup	25 mL
FILLING		
⅔ cup	seedless raspberry jam	150 mL

← Grease sides of 13- x 9-inch (3.5 L) metal cake pan; line bottom with parchment paper. Set aside.

← In large bowl, beat butter with sugar until light. Beat in eggs, 1 at a time, beating well after each addition; beat in vanilla. In separate bowl, sift together flour, cocoa powder, baking powder, baking soda and salt; sift again to completely blend. Stir into butter mixture alternately with buttermilk, making 3 additions of dry ingredients and 2 of buttermilk. Scrape into prepared pan, smoothing top.

←365

← Bake in centre of 350°F (180°C) oven until cake tester inserted in centre comes out clean, about 40 minutes. Let cool in pan on rack for 10 minutes. Invert onto rack; let cool completely. *Make-ahead: Wrap in plastic wrap and store at room temperature for up to 24 hours.*

← **CHOCOLATE GLAZE:** In heatproof bowl over saucepan of hot (not boiling) water, melt together chocolate, butter and corn syrup, stirring. Let cool until firm enough to spread, about 5 minutes.

← **FILLING:** Place cake on flat cake plate; cut in half horizontally. Spread cut side of bottom with raspberry jam; replace top half. Spread thin layer of chocolate glaze over top and side to mask; let stand until firm, about 5 minutes.

← Spread remaining glaze smoothly over cake; let stand until set, about 2 hours at room temperature or 1 hour in refrigerator. *Make-ahead: Cover with cake dome or plastic wrap; refrigerate for up to 24 hours. Let stand at room temperature for 20 minutes before serving.*

PER EACH OF 32 SERVINGS: about 263 cal, 4 g pro, 15 g total fat (9 g sat. fat), 32 g carb, 2 g fibre, 50 mg chol, 235 mg sodium.

% RDI: 4% calcium, 10% iron, 10% vit A, 2% vit C, 10% folate.

BEST
BUTTER TARTS

366 →

Whether runny or firm, with raisins or nuts, butter tarts are treats that never go out of style. Because any sugar filling that overflows the pastry hardens quickly and sticks to the pan, be sure to remove the tarts as directed. Or count on family members to hang around in the kitchen waiting to eat the tarts that stick and break.

Makes 12 tarts

1½ cups	all-purpose flour	375 mL
¼ tsp	salt	1 mL
¼ cup	cold butter, cubed	50 mL
¼ cup	lard or butter, cubed	50 mL
1	egg yolk	1
1 tsp	vinegar	5 mL
	Ice water	
FILLING		
½ cup	packed brown sugar	125 mL
½ cup	corn syrup	125 mL
1	egg	1
2 tbsp	butter, softened	25 mL
1 tsp	each vanilla and vinegar	5 mL
Pinch	salt	Pinch
¼ cup	currants, raisins, chopped pecans or shredded coconut	50 mL

← In large bowl, whisk flour with salt. With pastry blender or 2 knives, cut in butter and lard until mixture resembles coarse crumbs with a few larger pieces.

← In liquid measure, whisk egg yolk with vinegar; add enough ice water to make ⅓ cup (75 mL). Sprinkle over flour mixture, stirring briskly with fork until pastry holds together. Press into disc; wrap in plastic wrap and refrigerate until chilled, about 1 hour. *Make-ahead: Refrigerate for up to 3 days.*

← **FILLING:** In bowl, whisk together brown sugar, corn syrup, egg, butter, vanilla, vinegar and salt until blended; set aside.

← On lightly floured surface, roll out pastry to ⅛-inch (3 mm) thickness. Using 4-inch (10 cm) round cookie cutter (or empty 28 oz/796 mL can), cut out 12 circles, rerolling scraps once if necessary. Fit into 2¾- x 1¼-inch (7 x 3 cm) muffin cups. Divide currants among shells. Spoon in filling until three-quarters full.

← Bake in bottom third of 450°F (230°C) oven until filling is puffed and bubbly and pastry is golden, about 12 minutes. Let stand on rack for 1 minute. Run metal spatula around tarts to loosen; carefully slide spatula under tarts and transfer to rack to let cool.

PER TART: about 233 cal, 2 g pro, 11 g total fat (6 g sat. fat), 32 g carb, 1 g fibre, 55 mg chol, 133 mg sodium. % RDI: 2% calcium, 8% iron, 7% vit A, 5% vit C, 11 folate.

❧

VARIATIONS

CHOCOLATE GOOEY BUTTER TARTS

Drizzle cooled tarts with 2 oz (60 g) melted semisweet or white chocolate.

NOT-SO-GOOEY BUTTER TARTS

Increase brown sugar to ¾ cup (175 mL); decrease corn syrup to ¼ cup (50 mL).

APPLE PIE MUFFINS

Crusty-topped fruity muffins are spectacular weekend breakfast or brunch treats.

Makes 16 muffins

2¼ cups	all-purpose flour	550 mL
1½ cups	packed brown sugar	375 mL
1 tsp	baking soda	5 mL
½ tsp	salt	2 mL
1	egg	1
1 cup	buttermilk	250 mL
½ cup	butter, melted	125 mL
1 tsp	vanilla	5 mL
2 cups	diced peeled apples	500 mL

TOPPING

½ cup	packed brown sugar	125 mL
½ cup	chopped pecans	125 mL
⅓ cup	all-purpose flour	75 mL
1 tsp	cinnamon	5 mL
2 tbsp	butter, melted	25 mL

← Grease or line large muffin cups with paper liners; set aside.

← **TOPPING:** In bowl, stir together brown sugar, pecans, flour and cinnamon; drizzle with butter, tossing with fork. Set aside.

← In large bowl, whisk together flour, sugar, baking soda and salt. In separate bowl, whisk together egg, buttermilk, butter and vanilla; pour over dry ingredients. Sprinkle with apples; stir just until dry ingredients are moistened.

← Spoon into prepared cups; sprinkle with topping. Bake in centre of 375°F (190°C) oven until tops are firm to the touch, about 25 minutes. Let cool in pan on rack for 2 minutes. Run metal spatula around tarts to loosen; transfer to rack and let cool.

PER MUFFIN: about 286 cal, 3 g pro, 11 g total fat (5 g sat. fat), 46 g carb, 1 g fibre, 35 mg chol, 249 mg sodium. % RDI: 5% calcium, 12% iron, 7% vit A, 2% vit C, 13% folate.

TIP

If you don't have any buttermilk, pour 1 tbsp (25 mL) white vinegar into a measuring cup and add enough milk to make 1 cup (250 mL). Stir and let stand for 5 to 10 minutes and use as buttermilk.

370 →

— MICHAEL ALBERSTAT

Pages 19, 29, 67, 68, 71, 79, 88, 92, 108, 111, 113, 116, 133, 142, 164, 185, 190, 203, 211, 217, 227, 271, 302, 306, 336, 365

— FRED BIRD

Pages 326, 333, 369

— DOUGLAS BRADSHAW

Page 323

— YVONNE DUIVENVOORDEN

Pages 15, 17, 25, 26, 30, 41, 44, 45, 47, 49, 50, 53, 55, 56, 59, 73, 75, 76, 81, 82, 84, 85, 87, 91, 101, 102, 105, 106, 115, 122, 125, 126, 128, 131, 140, 144, 149, 153, 154, 156, 167, 168, 169, 171, 173, 174, 179, 183, 186, 188, 189, 194, 199, 200, 201, 204, 206, 208, 212, 214, 215, 219, 220, 223, 224, 230, 233, 241, 242, 244, 247, 249, 250, 253, 255, 256, 262, 265, 274, 276, 277, 279, 287, 290, 293, 296, 298, 301, 305, 311, 341, 343, 351, 352, 353, 355, 357, 353, 360, 361, 363 and all photos appearing on back cover

— ROB FIOCCA

Pages 119, 177, 259, 295

— PETE GAFFNEY

Page 315

— DONNA GRIFFITH

Pages 38, 43

— KEVIN HEWITT

Pages 121, 146, 151, 180, 267

— JERRY HUMENY

Page 23

— JO-ANNE MCARTHUR

Page 260

— MARC MONTPLAISIR

Chapter openers

— VINCENT NOGUCHI

Pages 334, 366

— ED O'NEIL

Page 268

— EDWARD POND

Pages 197, 273, 317

— DAVID SCOTT

Pages 193, 228, 312

— CURTIS TRENT

Pages 289, 338

— ROBERT WIGINGTON

Pages 20, 309, 324, 330

Special thanks go to the food stylists who helped make these photographs look so appetizing: Julie Aldis; Donna Bartolini; Ruth Gangbar; Sue Henderson; Jennifer McLagan; Lucie Richard; Claire Stancer; Claire Stubbs; Olga Truchan.

Integral to each of these photographs are the resourceful folks who find and style the props: Marc-Philippe Gagné; Miriam Gee; Jane Hardin; Maggi Jones; Catherine MacFadyen; Lara McGraw; Chareen Parsons; Suzie Routh; Oksana Slavutych; Janet Walkinshaw.

INDEX

ABOUT OUR NUTRITION INFORMATION

To meet nutrient needs each day, moderately active women 25 to 49 need about 1,900 calories, 51 g protein, 261 g carbohydrate, 25 to 35 g fibre and not more than 63 g total fat (21 g saturated fat). Men and teenagers usually need more. Canadian sodium intake of approximately 3,500 to 4,500 mg daily should be reduced. Percentage of recommended daily intake (% RDI) is based on the highest recommended intakes (excluding those for pregnant and lactating women) for calcium, iron, vitamins A and C, and folate. Figures are rounded off. They are based on the first ingredient listed when there is a choice and do not include optional ingredients.

ABBREVIATIONS

cal = calories
pro = protein
carb = carbohydrate
sat. fat = saturated fat
chol = cholesterol

ABOUT OUR RECIPES

The Canadian Living Test Kitchen, which includes associate food editor Gabrielle Bright, manager Heather Howe and staff members Kate Dowhan, Alison Kent, Kathy Lee Morren and James Smith, with assistant Christine Grimes, created all recipes in *Everyday Favourites* with the exception of the ones by these contributors:

— JULIE ALDIS

Butterscotch Apple Spice Cake (page 289) and Pork Tenderloin with Mushrooms Stuffing and Pan-Seared Onion and Apples (page 338)

— AFGHAN WOMEN'S CATERING

Baked Eggplant with Yogurt Sauce (page 273)

— DENNIS HELMUTH AND JOAN YODDER

Ruby Red Borscht (page 23)

We gratefully acknowledge their contribution.

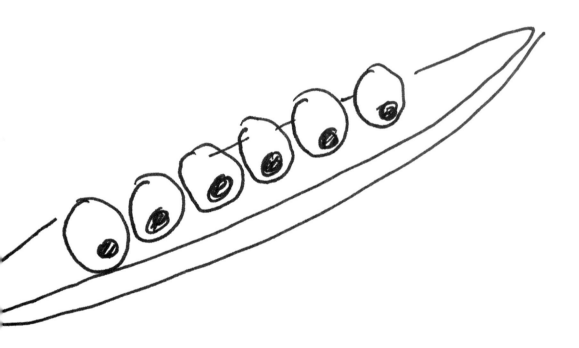